Advance Praise for
Behind Every Good Decision

"A solid analytical foundation is the basis for numerous emerging trends, and it is fundamental for any company to perform at its peak. *Behind Every Good Decision* will gently bring the neophyte into the analytical fold, show managers how to work with their analysts to get the most out of them, and create a framework that can make any business understand what drives its success and failures. A necessary read for any business leader, present or future."

—Brian Whalen, CFO, GiveCorps

"Thought provoking. Relevant. A practitioner's handbook. This book fills the gap between theory and practice of analytics with smart frameworks and solutions. Analytics experts and business managers often talk different languages. Then there is the added complexity of ever-increasing volumes of data and changing business models. This book provides good recipes and great insights to overcome this. Highly recommended for anyone who is looking to drive decisions with data."

**—Shekar Nalle Pilli Venkateswara (NV), Sr. Director,
Human Capital Analytics at Marriott International**

"As my grandfather used to say, "If you don't have time to do it right the first time, how will you find time to do it twice?" Following the process in this book will get you to the right question, the right model to analyze the data, and lead you to the right insights and recommendations—the first time. *Behind Every Good Decision* is a great book for business leaders, scientists, and nonanalytical professionals trying to solve everyday problems from deciding where to look for criminals, to finding out why sales are dropping off in a certain area, to deciding what car to buy. The many great examples and stories make it easy to understand. The chapter on common pitfalls holds up a mirror when skipping steps to cut corners or save time. I highly recommend this book for everyone in a business environment."

—**John C. Cummings, Managing Director,**
Applied Global Services

"A well-researched, thorough, and incredibly insightful book with great real-life examples. Enormously helpful to newbies and seasoned analytics professionals alike."

—**Sumit C. Kumar, Director, Global Marketing,**
Customer & Marketing Analytics Gap, Inc.

"*Behind Every Good Decision* provides a necessary and refreshing view of analytics and insight generation. Piyanka and Puneet have done a remarkable job putting the 'process' of analytics into perspective. The book delivers on its promise to guide readers how to apply business analytics and methodology to provide actionable insights, without too much focusing on data and technology. It is the right blend of people, process, technology, and strategy. Using examples, they tell stories of successes, and those of failures, to learn from organizations that have mastered business analytics as well as those that have fallen victim to gut-based decision making.

"BADIR is simple, easy to understand, and can be implemented in any organization. It delivers on the promise that analytics needn't rely on a technology or tool, and can be applied to all analyses using intuition and the right data. *Behind Every Good Decision* is a must-read for anyone involved in decision making, data analysis, and supporting their organization in getting to the next level."

—**Mike Lempner, Practice Executive,**
Business Intelligence and Big Data at Infinitive

"I have not come across any other page-turner in analytics. Concepts, terminology, and methodologies that even confound experts are translated into a very easy-to-grasp and interesting read. I highly recommend this to not just leaders, analysts, and consultants, but also to anyone who wants to improve operations in almost any field."
—**Mayank Jain, VP (Senior Business Leader),**
Workforce Planning, Visa

"*Behind Every Good Decision* is a must-read for business and technology professionals aiming to create a data-driven culture at work."
—**Jo Maitland, Research Director, GigaOM**

"This book does an outstanding job of (a) re-emphasizing the necessity to analyze the ever-increasing amount of data created by the enterprise to remain competitive in the digital economy, (b) taking a targeted approach in its delivery of content to different audiences (analysts, managers, leaders), (c) dispelling the 'Ivory Tower' aspects of data analyses, providing clear guidance on the whens and whys of using a relatively simple set of actionable approaches that result in quick wins, and (d) underscoring the importance of the soft skills required to incorporate analytics into decision making."
—**Christiaan Berge, Vice President**
at RoundPoint Financial Group

"*Behind Every Good Decision* is a much-needed desktop guide to problem solving. Summarizing all that any analytics professional needs to go from insights to strategy, it is for all levels of management. The BADIR framework gets us from a hypothesis to actionable results that lead to a positive change.

"This book gives a solid overview of simple analysis techniques and complex predictive analytics in a single place with great examples, something that has not been done before. A must-have guide for all those who work in analytics, and for those who want to start learning it."
—**Mihir Korke, VP, Swift Capital**

"*Behind Every Good Decision* is a very engrossing and interesting read. As the digital age generates thousands of terabytes of data every day, driving insights from data results in a huge competitive advantage. As a business leader, I have seen many data analysts who are great at number-crunching but who fail in grasping the right business context. This book is a must-read for all budding analysts to understand the potential of their roles in driving the success of their organizations, and keeping it smart and simple. Analytics is still in its development stages as a strategic business lever. *Behind Every Good Decision* is also great for business leaders to understand how to effectively leverage analytics to quickly generate insights into business problems. Kudos to Piyanka and Puneet."

—Anshul Mohan, Head of Sales for North America–
Energy, Communications & Services at Infosys BPO

"*Behind Every Good Decision* is a must-read for both newly minted college graduates wanting to peek into the magical world of business analytics, and business veterans who want to increase the effectiveness of their organizations by further leveraging the power of analytics. In an age where all good decisions are increasingly driven by data and analytics, Piyanka and Puneet show how successful companies in many different fields are ushering a new way of doing business."

—Kemal Karakaya, Manager at PwC Advisory

"*Behind Every Good Decision* is a simple yet application-oriented guide to data analytics—essential for a better interpretation of the opportunities at hand and the icebergs that lie ahead. I highly recommend reading it."

—Abhishek Darbari, Senior Vice President,
Group Risk Management, UniCredit Spa

BEHIND EVERY
GOOD DECISION

How Anyone Can Use Business Analytics to Turn Data into Profitable Insight

PIYANKA JAIN
&
PUNEET SHARMA

EDITED BY

Lakshmi Jayaraman

HARPERCOLLINS
LEADERSHIP

AN IMPRINT OF HARPERCOLLINS

For bulk discounts, please visit:
https://www.harpercollinsleadership.com/bulk-sales/
Or contact us at
Email: hcleadership@harpercollins.com
Phone: 1-800-250-5308

© 2015 Piyanka Jain and Puneet Sharma

All rights reserved. No portion of this book may be reproduced, stored in a retrieval system, or transmitted in any form or by any means --electronic, mechanical, photocopy, recording, scanning, or other --except for brief quotations in critical reviews or articles, without the prior written permission of the publisher.

Published by HarperCollins Leadership, an imprint of HarperCollins Focus LLC.

Any internet addresses, phone numbers, or company or product information printed in this book are offered as a resource and are not intended in any way to be or to imply an endorsement by HarperCollins Leadership, nor does HarperCollins Leadership vouch for the existence, content, or services of these sites, phone numbers, companies, or products beyond the life of this book.

ISBN 978-0-8144-4922-6 (eBook)
ISBN 978-0-8144-4921-9 (HC)
ISBN 978-1-4002-3104-1 (TP)

Library of Congress Cataloguing-in-Publication Data

Library of Congress Control Number: 2014014383

For Jia, the magic in my life;
Parth, my pillar of support;
and my parents, the source of my strength.

—PIYANKA JAIN

For Shweta, who always believes in me; and
my children, Nikhil and Samir, who bring joy to my life.

—PUNEET SHARMA

Contents

Preface

PIYANKA:

I hate statistics. What I really wanted to do in 1999, in an environmental engineering thesis at Texas A&M University, was to track events that caused a hazardous waste site to be, well, hazardous. While researching in the lab, I was frankly mortified as it became clear to me that the only way I could solve this was by building an inverse speciation model using nonlinear regression.

I have always loved numbers and math—having derived the Pythagorean theorem in my own fashion four years too early for my grade. I have always questioned the impact of every engineering feat, including my dad's breakthrough "waste-to-energy" invention. Math and engineering define me for what I am today, but in 1999, I worked to make sure that statistics could not only analyze a problem, but solve it, and have true tangible business impact. I had befriended the enemy, and found my passion.

For a second master's degree in computer engineering at the University of Minnesota, statistical modeling and simulation helped me design a self-updating network routing table using the concept of ant pheromones. I taught calculus and statistics to third- and fourth-year undergraduates. I now felt empowered to solve different types of problems with statistics and analytics.

When Adobe was looking for those skills to improve its customer experience, I knew analytics would be my life from this point forward. As always, I worked to make sure that my play with data was translated to action and positive consequences for the business. Within a data-loving organization, my team and I were able to impact the business through marketing, advertising, improved customer experiences, and eventually the company's bottom line.

As my career progressed at different companies, I met Puneet at PayPal, as we led an analytics group each within the company.

PUNEET:

My early career began with a computer science degree and an MBA in finance. But when I came to know of data, analytics, and a day in the life of my data analyst friends, I knew I had to succumb to that itch—what I refer to as my "Calling." When Capital One was looking for a data analyst, I applied. After passing the rigorous aptitude test, Capital One invited me on board as a data analytics manager to capitalize on my technology and business skills. Here I flourished in what I loved best—to translate analytics to business impact and to tangible dollar value. The company believed in having data inform all key strategies and decisions, and was designed this way from the ground up. I was trained along with 500 others to learn statistics, modeling, and analytics. I knew I had made the right decision to move into data analytics.

After this, however, I was surprised to learn that other companies I worked with weren't interested as much—or even at all—in leveraging data to drive business impact. Analytics was a "support function" whose outputs may or may not be considered, depending on the priorities of different business units. The systems weren't set up for us to gain the level of business context that could make a deep impact. Resources were being spent on theoretical analytics, but not always to drive direct business impact. In projects that had support from a strong data-driven executive, my team and I were able to deliver incredible impact. But where that wasn't the case, I was witnessing tens of millions of dollars lying untapped purely as a factor of the organizational structure and perceived value of analytics! Ouch! After a period of intense self-doubt about my capabilities to drive consistent impact, I saw it. There was a need. There was a gap, and I learned from those failures. These are lessons I still capitalize on as the analytics leader for a technology company.

Over years of lunches and talks, Piyanka and I saw that we were experiencing the same things. We started to see the patterns clearly and to figure ways to plug those gaps. It wasn't just about the analytics, but also about the environment where it can be quantifiably powerful to move the needle of the business. The complexity of analytics was a roadblock, but we knew that those resource intensive processes were only required about 20 percent of the time. Together, we started to articulate the power of analytics, the attitude of organizations toward analytics, common missteps, and simple role-agnostic methods to drive impact.

PIYANKA:

Over the years as I spoke at conferences, I heard firsthand experiences about data from compatriots in other organizations. They were overwhelmed—with data, Big Data, analytics, predictive analytics—and while many had jumped on the bandwagon, their investment in analytics wasn't delivering much return on investment (ROI). The whole scene was vague and complex. There was a need we could fill.

In 2011, I started Aryng, a management consulting firm focused on analytics. With Puneet in an advisory role, I developed a recipe for analytics for business impact. BADIR™, which stands for **B**usiness question, **A**nalysis plan, **D**ata collection, **I**nsights, and **R**ecommendations, is a simple five-step framework for turning data into smarter decisions.

As we were conducting workshops, we heard more and more that such a simple bite-size and commonsensical approach to analytics wasn't available to industry and academia. This book is an encapsulation of all of this. We're delighted to take you along on this journey.

Acknowledgments

This book is a culmination of our beliefs and knowledge of business analytics. While it has taken over our lives during the last several months, it simply could not have come to fruition without the help and support of our friends and family members, who not only generously contributed their varied expertise, but also generously tolerated us on this journey. We feel grateful to have the support of these compassionate and highly intelligent individuals.

We're analytics experts—not writers. Thank you Lakshmi Jayaraman for giving this book a voice with your tireless work in telling our story, adding design and innovation context, and writing and editing. We also thank you just as much for your insistence on making it fun and readable through your design expertise and help with the illustrations.

A very special thanks to our reviewers whose feedback ensured we made sense and were clearly communicating the intent of the content. So thank you Bonny Elgamil, Claire Dean, Nirmal Baid, Desmond Chan, Marcia Trask, Ketan Babaria, Parth Sethia, Sangita Khater, Sunil Bafna, Anshul Mohan, Mahendra Kumar, Narasimman Jayaraman, Kamala Subramaniam, Cole Roberts, and Betty Li.

Thank you Ramkumar Ravichandran for your research and review of analytics and data tools; Kameshwari Viswanadha, for your design input and review; and Vijay Aviur, for contributing to stories that we have included in this book.

Thank you Shailesh, Ashish, and the Satvik team for the illustrations that have made this book come alive. Thank you Terri Griffith for your insight into the book writing process and the many introductions you enabled.

Finally, we want to acknowledge the support we had from our families and specifically our respective spouses, Parth and Shweta, who took on many roles while we hid in the study most days, or disappeared most weekends.

Introduction

Nothing is rocket science except, well, rocket science. The corollary is true: Analytics is not rocket science. Sure, it is a specialized subject involving megaloads of information in every conceivable format, and we spend millions trying to find patterns through analysis—with some human insight, simple math, and complex statistics. Okay, that sounds hard, but just as with any subject you begin to understand, there are fundamentals, methods, and simple tricks to master it and use it for your own benefit. Albeit with a complex component, analytics—business analytics—is actually a simple problem-solving tool, and *Behind Every Good Decision* was written to describe what it is, and how it is so.

We've told you analytics can be simple. Have we told you that everyone in your organization can know enough to effect positive change in your organization on a day-to-day basis? Or that simple analytics can actually help you solve 80 percent of your business problems at a fraction of the cost of complex analytics? Well, it can.

Not all analytics problems need to be megacomplex projects with complex models built and read by a data scientist. In fact, 80 percent of these problems can be addressed day to day by managers and decision makers who have had the right exposure to simple tools and methods. They will know when and how best to leverage data scientists and analysts to solve more complex business issues. This book is designed to prime these business professionals with the basics and help data scientists deliver at their best. It seeks to marry the best of both worlds to drive results.

So what kind of results is analytics expected to influence? Done correctly, analytics can discover gaps in organizations and create happy customers, better products, streamlined processes, productive employees, improved revenue and profits, and therefore, happier shareholders. What we have seen in our combined 30 years of experience leading analytics in large corporations is that some do it right, and others struggle. The pattern became apparent to us. With organizational trust in analytics, informed resources, clear communication, and simple methods, successful organizations have been able to leverage analytics to drive growth. The ones that struggle take different missteps, but have a simple way out—and that is what this book is about.

Each time there is a hot buzzword, companies jump on the bandwagon in a hurry. Knowing its potential to deliver obvious value, organizations start with a scramble of misplaced expectations with analytics (and Big Data, too). They believe analytics is just too complex. It needs "scientists," who can solve all problems in their data labs. They think data should spill out answers periodically and that a Big Data tool will fix it all. . . . No, no, no, no, and no! We hope to dispel these and other misconceptions.

But how do you break from this analysis paralysis? There is a method to this madness, and our commonsensical BADIR™ framework (see Chapter 4) will help you get from Data to Decisions™ in five simple steps. This method is so universal that it is applicable to a wide cross-section of businesses and industries. We've included such examples throughout the book to illustrate this point.

These examples came from our individual experiences working as part of or heading analytics teams within large corporations in Silicon Valley and recently through Aryng.

WHO IS THIS BOOK FOR?

For everyone: Sections I, III, and IV are for everyone interested in knowing about analytics. Section I is an introduction to analytics: the what, why, and common methodologies. Section III is about building a data-driven organization. Section IV contains real-life stories on how analytics has catapulted typical business environments—from politics to sports to law enforcement to technology.

For people who want to learn hands-on analytics: Section II delves into BADIR for business analytics in detail, providing an overview of predictive analytics and introducing tools used in business intelligence and analytics. This section will equip you with the necessary knowledge to apply business analytics to most of your day-to-day situations and to engage adequately with specialists for complex analytics when required. A brief primer in statistics is available in the Appendix.

For leaders: Business leaders as well as analytics leaders will find Section III worthwhile, as you lead your organization up the remunerative path to be data empowered. It has a toolkit and proprietary methodologies to help you create a data-enabled organization, to set up an analytics agenda, to amplify the impact of analytics in a cross-functional organization, and to avoid common pitfalls.

LINGO TO GO

We've used the following terms throughout the book; it would help you to be familiar with them, so we are defining them here.

A/B Testing or Test and Learn: Testing is the process of gauging the validity of insights generated from analytics, intuition, or customer input. It evaluates the performance of these insights in a controlled experiment.

Analytics: The science of applying a structured method to solve a business problem using data and analysis to drive impact.

BADIR: An easy-to-follow recipe to move from Data to Decisions. It combines data science with decision science (i.e., technical skills with business and soft skills) to convert data into insights leading to impact. This process is industry agnostic. It is covered in Chapter 4.

Business Analytics: The application of simpler statistical methodologies to historical data, coupled with business context, to gain insights and drive impact in an organization. These include methodologies like correlation and aggregate analysis.

Business Leader: An individual in the leadership role of a function, business unit, or entire organization, including CEOs, General Managers, Heads of Product, Heads of Marketing, Heads of Customer Engagement. In these roles, they are responsible for the profit and loss (P&L) of their business unit and are critical in influencing the strategy of their company.

Business User or Business Professional: Anyone in any industry who executes on strategy and manages day-to-day decisions for his or her function that directly and indirectly influence the performance of the company. We use these terms interchangeably, and their functions could be in marketing, product, operations, or other roles.

Data Driven: Some companies are innovation driven; others are technology driven. A company that is data driven supports all these organizations in their respective goals, using data to drive better decisions. We use data enabled, data led and data driven as appropriate in this book. The reader can adopt whichever term supports his or her organization's vision and goals.

Data Scientist: An individual with the ability to do advanced analytics using advanced statistical tools. Used interchangeably with "Analytics Professional."

KPI: A key performance indicator is a measure of success for any organization or a project. Revenue and margins are often the KPIs at the organization level.

P&L: Profit and loss.

Predictive Analytics: The application of advanced statistical techniques to historical data to predict future events. This includes techniques like regression and decision trees. These usually require the expertise of data scientists and predictive analytics professionals.

3 Key Questions™: Another Aryng recipe to lay an actionable analytics agenda for an organization. 3 Key Questions is a methodology leaders can use to start peeling the onion of their business by nailing down the KPIs, finding the drivers of those KPIs, and aligning internal projects to move the drivers that impact the KPIs.

1

HELLO ANALYTICS!

ONE

Analytics or Die

THIS CHAPTER WILL TALK ABOUT:

Why analytics? Because you can't depend on chance.

What is analytics?

Circuit City,[1] a dominant big box electronic retailer in the United States, grew throughout the 1980s and 1990s, as it established an empire of stores in strategic locations from coast to coast. In August 2008, Circuit City's biggest rival, Best Buy, reported increased sales and a quarterly profit of $200 million. That same quarter, Circuit City reported a loss of $239 million.[2] On March 9, 2009, Circuit City shuttered the last of its 567 retail stores.

The magic had ended. But what had happened?

In the late 1990s, growth of web commerce was projected at 2300 percent. Best Buy brought its website to the world in 2000. Circuit City didn't.

In 1999, Circuit City announced $1.6 billion in annual sales revenue from large appliances, second only to Sears. In 2000, it decided to stop selling appliances to save on warehouse storage and delivery costs. The housing boom of the mid-2000s saw the largest home appliance sales since the mid-1800s, when home appliances first appeared. Circuit City had missed the wave.

By 2004, Best Buy had secured "A" quality locations, whereas Circuit City opted for low-cost leases in distant locations to save on rent. Consumers flocked to stores they could get to in a 10-minute car ride.

Circuit City let go of its highest paid sales personnel from local stores to reduce the cost of manpower, while maintaining the employee head count in stores. Many of these well-paid sales associates were the company's best, generating the greatest revenue, and most loyal, having stayed through the company's growing pains. They took their skills and experience to Best Buy and other competitors.[2]

Many strategic missteps contribute to the fall of any corporate giant. The factors above are those that could have been addressed through the power of data analytics. Keeping an eye on growth projections from the industry and a competitor's adoption of emerging technologies would have informed Circuit City to boost its online presence. In deciding to cut costs, an ROI analysis would have stopped the company from firing its highest paid employees who were bringing in disproportionately higher revenue. If Circuit City had analyzed the data to balance supply and demand to inform its inventory management, its leaders wouldn't have undertaken these illogical cost-cutting exercises to cover the debt from unsold inventory. Management made two critical decisions company-wide to reduce costs: (1) to close its appliance business and (2) to move its retail locations to "B," or suburban, locations. Data may have indicated that this is where the main costs lie, but the decisions were not properly tested. Reducing appliance inventory and observing the performance of a few test stores in the "B" locations first would have disproved these strategies, saving the company from closing its lucrative appliance business and moving into the suburbs, thereby losing its clientele.

Analytics is not just about data, but about decisions. If Circuit City had leveraged data analytics effectively and made good decisions based on them, the company might still be in business.

WHAT IS ANALYTICS?

Analytics is the science of applying a structured method to solve a business problem using data and analysis to drive impact. Many businesses grapple with strategic business problems like cost cutting and business innovation. Initiatives to tackle such problems tend to shake up budgets and organizational structures. Data analytics can be a powerful tool in these decisions. The right analytics approach is an informed solution backed by data and insights.

Intuition + Data = Powerful insights → Good decision

Not just insights, but *actionable* insights—the kind that promote new thought processes, drive decision making, and impel positive action. Industry leaders like Procter & Gamble, Amazon, LinkedIn, and Capital One have dominated their fields by deploying data-led, hypothesis-driven, and analytics-powered strategies backed by vision and intuition. We will talk about these methods in this book.

Welcome to the world of business analytics.

> *The year 2011 saw Procter & Gamble record over $82.6 billion in sales.[3] Fortune magazine placed P&G at fifth place on the "World's Most Admired Companies" list, up from sixth place the previous year.*

With 127,000 employees worldwide and 300 brands sold in 180 countries, how has P&G managed to lead the household goods industry over the 177 years of its existence—since 1837? This $140 billion conglomerate consumer goods company has contextually reinvented itself over time using a *hypothesis-driven analytics strategy* to stay relevant and fuel the edge.

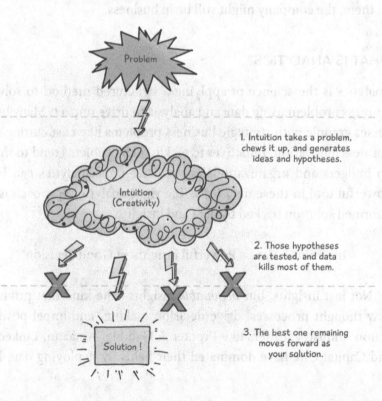

Problem

1. Intuition takes a problem, chews it up, and generates ideas and hypotheses.

Intuition
(Creativity)

2. Those hypotheses are tested, and data kills most of them.

Solution !

3. The best one remaining moves forward as your solution.

What is *hypothesis-driven analytics*? Imagine swimming the Pacific Ocean to find gold. Wouldn't you rather narrow down the most likely areas where gold could be, so you wouldn't have to cover every square inch of water from China to America?

Similarly, data is an ocean, and hypotheses help to narrow down where to find the most likely answers. Hypotheses are generated by human intuition based on the collective intelligence and experience of stakeholders and their understanding of the business and their environment. Data validates the hypotheses to come up with a convergent solution. The strength of the solution then will lie in the best of both—data and hypotheses.

How does hypothesis-driven analytics strategy work?

It starts with answering a set of plain sounding questions, "What is happening?" and "Why is it happening?" These simple questions have helped companies like P&G identify actions that can be taken to address a situation. Action without insight means decisions are made without any perspective on which paths would yield results.

In 2010, P&G CEO Bob McDonald strategized to digitize the company's processes end-to-end to achieve business optimization and decision efficiency using analytics. But P&G was simultaneously tasked with cutting costs. By 2012, it had eliminated 1,600 nonmanufacturing jobs, and its IT organization had cut over $900 million in total expenditure. Despite reducing headcount and expenses, P&G managed to score an increase in gross revenue.

How? P&G invested in analytics expertise to develop its capabilities to make wise and timely decisions in unpredictable and stressful environments.[4] Its analytics provided predictions about P&G market share and other performance statistics up to a year into the future. At the core of this capability was a series of analytic models that reveal events in the business as they occur, including peaks and valleys in performance, identify reasons why they occur, and point to actions P&G can take to leverage or mitigate effects from these events.

P&G's analytics is driven by a cultural mindset to ask questions and propose hypotheses before delving into complex data analytics. "What" monitors areas like shipments, sales, and market share to keep an eye on the key metrics for the business. When exceptions occur, "Why" drills down to the drivers—country, territory, product line, and store levels—to understand the specifics behind what is happening. Analytics then identifies "action levers" that P&G can pull, such as pricing, advertising, and product mix, and provides estimates of what that action can potentially deliver. By efficiently establishing the whats and the whys, decision makers at P&G have been able to jump right into solving a problem, radically increasing efficiency and the pace of conducting business.

This strategy surely works for giants like P&G. Now, how can *You*, facing an ever-shrinking budget and ever-brimming datasets, take on your company's health and prosperity like the goliaths of the industry? How can you execute your business strategy with optimal efficiency and make the smartest business decisions possible?

You can, by asking the right sets of "Whats" and "Hows" and by using a simple structured process—a hypothesis-driven analysis, followed by testing of insights—identify strategies to implement.

Data doesn't speak.
It responds.

It isn't rocket science, but rather a commonsensical secret. Like P&G, just ask these plain questions through the hypothesis-driven data-led process outlined below (see Exhibit 1-1). A hypotheses-driven analytics strategy can provide significant benefits, including greater insight and faster time to information and actions. The actionable insights generated from a hypotheses-driven approach are precise enough to allow for clear implementation.

A complete hypothesis-driven process is illustrated in the figure below.

EXHIBIT 1-1. Hypotheses-Driven Analytics Strategies: Whats and Hows

{ INTENT } *"What are you trying to do?"* OR *"What is happening that is not supposed to happen?"*	The very answer to that seemingly simple question establishes the **intent of your initiative**. Boom. It sets the context and aligns your thoughts in the direction of the desired goal. It provides the basis and rationale for optimization and effective transformation, and thereby drives the motivation for your strategy and actions. This question also helps you get to the root of a problem or pressing issue that needs immediate attention and effective resolution. It also helps you identify various contributors and, more important, obstacles to success. The answers will open the right gates for you to peek inside and explore more.
{ HYPOTHESES } *"What could drive it?"* OR *"Why is it happening?"*	Answer this question and you now know your **potential catalysts and key drivers**. The answer to the question can help identify key stakeholders and initiatives. The important thing to remember is that the answer to this question is not definitive—it is still a hypothesis. But it is the best clue you've got to make your best bet to start solving the problem at hand.
{ ANALYSIS } *"We could do A or B or C or D to solve this."* *"Based on analysis, doing A and B will likely increase margin."*	Then you do analysis to prove or disprove hypotheses with data and find actionable insights. The insights show you the levers you need to pull, what initiatives you need to stop, and what action you need to take to address the question at hand. For additional information on how this works, see Chapter 4.

{ TESTING }

"Analysis says B can increase our margins by X percent and A by Y percent."
"Testing with consumers tells us, they simply love B."

To reinforce the actionability of the insights, it is important to test those insights for early learning and before final execution. Consumers play a key role in determining the viability of a product and its prospective future sales. While you may have uncovered a need for a product feature using the "what and why" and the insights may support your hypotheses, it is prudent to design a trial product to demonstrate ideas and capabilities to potential groups of customers (as with a test roll out to a customer segment) to see if you were right on both counts.

A NEW NORMAL

Here's a bold statement. Every company is exposed to the very same factors to virtually the same degree. It is not the challenge that distinguishes the success of an organization, but its *response* to the challenge. Companies that ride the economic and competitive tsunamis with ease can survive and thrive. On the other hand, bad internal decisions made in response to market challenges can weaken a company to the point of collapse.

The reality of a weakened economy since 2008 and its limp, slow recovery has complicated business worldwide. The effects of plummeting sales, shrinking budgets, and demanding customers have elicited varied reactions from organizations—some made smarter decisions and rode the waves, while others drowned in the wake. That said, numerous factors contribute to the success or failure of an organization. Intense pressures from external market conditions can impede profitability. The rise and fall of consumer confidence, investments, and economic turmoil can create overwhelming obstacles. Competition and rapidly emerging technology can wreak havoc on the best-laid plans. This landscape is forcing a paradigm shift in tools and approach to business problems.

Analytics is your key to making smarter decisions based on your very specific internal business dynamics. Not surprising is that a recent study based on data from 60 case studies found that analytics pays back $10.66 for every dollar spent.[5]

"But really, is analytics for me? Can analytics help me double my business with a shrinking budget?" Yes and yes.

ANALYTICS IS FOR EVERYBODY

Yes—everyone from daily managers to leaders to scientists to one looking to buy a car. If you aspire to run your business with maximum efficiency and effectiveness and make the smartest business decisions possible, if you are part of an enterprise whose tolerance for decision error is getting slimmer by the day, if you are looking for new sources of advantage and differentiation for your enterprise, if you are struggling in a highly complex global environment with increasing competition, expedited time to market, and highly selective customers, if you nurture any hopes of increasing your business in spite of all external challenges and an ever-shrinking budget, and even if you're just looking to buy a car, then it is time for you to say hello to analytics.

Analytics pays back
$10.66 for every dollar spent.

IN A NUTSHELL

- Analytics is not just about data, but about decisions.
- There is a method to the madness: It starts with asking the right "Whats" and "Hows."
- Analytics is for everyone.

What Is Analytics?

Scene 1

You are Ben, the Quality Control Manager at Bright Sun Solar Cell Manufacturing Company, and you have just received a note from your testing group that the last batch of solar panels has had an alarmingly low rate of product efficiency. With your reputation at stake, you need to move full throttle into action to understand what went wrong. Questions race through your mind. "Why was there such a high failure rate on the last batch?" "How will we fix it?" "How can I ensure that future batches don't have the same problem?"

The clock is ticking. Each incremental failure adds to the revenue losses already incurred, costs that are creeping into the millions.

Scene 2

You are Andreas, a treasure hunter, the Captain of the Moon Princess. Your dream is about to come true. A private investor has just offered you a large grant to search for lost treasures in the Pacific Ocean. Better yet, she offered you a special bonus if you find the sunken 1715 shipwreck, dubbed "Plate Fleet" for the silver plates on board.[1]

But the grant is only sufficient to cover you and your crew for 30 days at sea.

WILL YOU BE CHRISTOPHER COLUMBUS OR SHERLOCK HOLMES?

We'll start by saying that in these two very different situations, treasure hunting and solving manufacturing defects, the path to the solution, actually the efficient solution, would be very similar.

If you were like Christopher Columbus, you might set sail into the ocean with your crew and submarine in tow and just start looking for the treasure wherever it lay. This would be an enjoyable route and you would, no doubt, find yourself enthralled with the sublime beauty of the ocean—the shimmering green waters, the dolphins leaping playfully in your wake, and the ancient, remarkable coral reefs.

Meanwhile, the clock is ticking on your grant money. Are you  doing it as efficiently and expeditiously as possible? In 30 days, will you have found the *Plate Fleet*? Probably not, as your actions of exploration are independent of your goal to find the *Plate Fleet*. Had you been tasked to look for killer whales or a kind of edible seaweed, your actions might have been exactly the same. You have taken the explorer approach.

Now, if you were like Sherlock Holmes, what would you do? You might identify potential areas where shipwrecks have occurred and research specifically where the *Plate Fleet* may have sunk. You might look at historical trade routes and records of wrecks. Then, using depth information, you would eliminate possibilities. And, you don't want just any shipwreck; you want to pinpoint where the *Plate Fleet* sank. You would look at the records of 1715 hurricane paths. By using clues and facts, you would begin to identify potential areas where the treasure could be found. Once you have identified a dozen or so potential locations and prioritized the top three, you would send your submarine or deep-sea divers down to investigate.

You have just multiplied your chances of finding the *Plate Fleet*, and in a much shorter time, just by engaging in a focused search based on appropriate information. Should you fail, you would still have time to strategize again and attack the problem again. This is the detective approach.

As Ben, your approach to identifying and fixing the problem that caused the solar panels to fail is no different than the treasure hunt. With Columbus's explorer approach, you could be collecting an incredible amount of data points in the hope of finding the cause of the failure. But, as you can imagine, with multiple assembly lines, each one with a multitude of processes and equipment, the chances of stumbling into the problem area quickly are going to be slim.

Maybe the problem is simply a single valve malfunction, but imagine the probability of finding it among the hundreds of things you would have to look at! Again, how lucky are you, and are you willing to trust your career to luck?

BEN, MEET DATA-DRIVEN DECISION MAKING

Play detective. Pore over the data to decipher the clues that will tell you what went wrong. This is Business Analytics 101. Start asking questions. Where did the failure happen? Are all the lines producing unusually faulty products, or was this an isolated incident? When did the problem start? Where exactly are the faults in the product and to what processes or equipment does it correspond? You get the gist.

The most important thing to note is this: You don't have to know all the answers to the guided questions you are asking. You can construct a solid hypothesis based on what you have already learned, partial as it may be, and then use that hypothesis to identify the most likely problem suspects.

By being Sherlock, you quickly discover that high temperatures in line ten caused the fault in the product. Temperature issues are often caused by raw material quality issues or by hardware, such as a malfunctioning heat exchanger. By identifying the top things to look for, you can easily narrow down the cause of the problem, which in this case is a faulty valve on a heat exchanger. You have saved time and resources getting to the root of the problem, and your supervisor recognizes you for it. At least that's what we hope!

IS IT ROCKET SCIENCE?

The word *analytics* does conjure up a vague image of a long complex equation from a statistics class, but analytics as applied to business is not that complex. The reality is that a very small number of statistical techniques learned in statistics class can actually be applied in a business scenario. From the techniques that can apply to a business problem, only a very small percentage meets the business constraints of ROI, explainability, maintainability, turnaround time, and scalability. So, simpler analysis techniques win hands down in a business situation.

In 2006, Netflix announced a data mining competition for a prize of $1 million to improve its movie rating prediction by 10 percent.[2] A classic business meets statistics scenario. A very large number of data miners competed. A year later, the progress prize winning team reported it had spent more than 2,000 hours to achieve an 8.43 percent improvement. Two years later, an ensemble (a combination of models) finally delivered the 10 percent improvement to qualify as the winner. The winning solution was a blend of hundreds of individual models, but Netflix is not using it. Why? Because the solution was operationally expensive to implement, and the gain in revenue from the better recommendation didn't offset the cost of scoring and maintaining the model.

As it turns out, the most useful analytics techniques in business are contained in a small set of simpler techniques that can be learned by most professionals. You'll also be surprised to know that it is actually the *people skills* needed for bridging the gap between business and math that make or break the deal.

ANALYTICS IN BUSINESS

Analytics is only useful when it drives impact. Depending on your business, impact can be revenue growth, process efficiency, and improved offerings.

Analytics for impact = Data science + Decision science

Analytics for impact has two components:

- **Data science:** This is the technical track, designed to derive insights from data.
- **Decision science:** This is the business track, designed to align stakeholders so that the valuable insights produced using the data science track can be inserted into the decision-making process and converted into action.

Great analytics is not just about cool and complex models. It is also about using soft skills, understanding the business, and presenting relevant insights useful in the context of business to drive business impact. Unless analytics drives business impact, it is not analytics. It is just statistics; it is just data science. Often, analysts get so mired in the data to focus on getting the coolest insights that they miss the human element.

A successful business analytics professional is not a statistician (although statisticians make great analysts), but someone who engages enthusiastically and appropriately with business counterparts who

approach them to perform data analysis. True, the analyst needs to choose the right technique for analysis and deliver insights. But a successful analyst uses influence and soft skills to build alignment with the stakeholders or business counterparts. This ensures that when the golden nuggets of insights are mined, the business counterpart is ready to act on it by turning those insights into business impact. More information on this will be presented in Chapter 4 and Chapter 10.

Using question-and-answer sessions with their counterparts, the successful analyst arrives at a crisper definition of what is being asked of the data (the real business question) and what might be some of the clues toward the answer (hypotheses). They can use these answers to dig into the right data, do the appropriate analysis, and make actionable recommendations.

This is not to say technical analysis and modeling skills are not important, but without the rudder of business and people skills, the ship becomes lost in the ocean.

THE 80:20 RULE OF ANALYTICS

The analytics landscape is still in its formative stage. So definitions and terminology are in flux and will probably remain so for some time. For the purpose of this book, we will use these terms:

Business analytics: The use of simpler analytics methodologies on past data.

Advanced analytics: Everything else, including predictive analytics.

With all the big talk about Big Data and predictive analytics—both of which involve complex skills and tools driving millions of dollars in marketing—it is hard to believe in the power of simple analytics. The truth, however, is that only 20 to 30 percent of decisions really require the use of advanced techniques like predictive analytics. Seventy to 80 percent of business decisions can be judiciously addressed with business analytics, or simple analytics techniques, which can be learned by any professional and executed in an Excel spreadsheet. Predictive analytics is an extension of business analytics. It uses understanding gained from analyzing historical data to predict future events or behavior. It can be employed to improve the accuracy of insights gained from business analytics (see Exhibit 2-1).

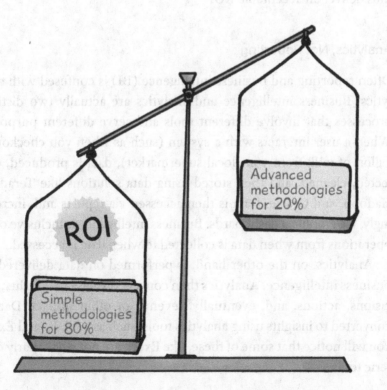

EXHIBIT 2-1. Pros and Cons of Business and Predictive Analytics

BUSINESS ANALYTICS	PREDICTIVE ANALYTICS
[+] Quick and easy.	[−] Time and resource intensive.
[+] Can be learned by most business professionals and done using common tools like Excel.	[−] Needs specialized modeling skills and advanced statistical tools.
[−] Not exhaustive, so may miss the top parameter that can drive the biggest business outcome.	[+] Can evaluate hundreds of metrics and can thus identify the most important parameters to drive biggest business outcomes.

We encourage the use of business analytics first in solving any business problem because it delivers strong ROI with limited effort. Subsequently, for a subset of problems, leverage advanced analytics where the expected returns can offset the high initial investment and thus deliver an acceptable ROI.

Analytics, Not Reporting

Often reporting and business intelligence (BI) is confused with analytics. Business intelligence and analytics are actually two distinct processes that involve different tools and serve different purposes. When a user interacts with a system (such as when you checkout a gallon of milk from your local supermarket), data is produced, collected, cleaned, and then stored using data solutions like Teradata, Hadoop, and Oracle. Data is then accessed via reports and, increasingly, via graphical dashboards. Business intelligence is inclusive of all operations from when data is collected to when data is accessed.

Analytics, on the other hand, is performed on data delivered by business intelligence. Analytics then convert the data to insights, decisions, actions, and, eventually, revenue or other impact. Data is converted to insights using analytics tools, such as SAS, R, and Excel. You will notice that some of these, like Excel, are not particularly esoteric tools.

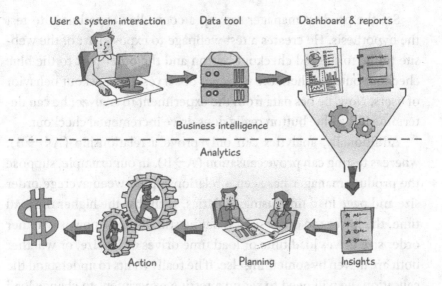

For example, a toy store may have a dashboard that tells the manager that revenues for the current week are down 10 percent from last week and the number of visitors is down 2 percent. Analysis will tell the story that numbers for a specific segment, like most frequent users, were 2 percent lower than last week. This indicates that the issue has something to do with the highly engaged users and will help the store manager focus on the related area of the business.

ANALYTICS VERSUS TESTING

Analytics looks at a business event and analyzes the historical data to come up with insights. Testing, on the other hand, is a controlled experiment conducted when you do not have historical data on which to base a decision. Take, for example, an ecommerce site that has a red checkout button. Based on focus group input, the product manager has a strong hypothesis that a blue checkout button would be preferred by users and could drive more checkout and conversion. However, the site has never had a blue checkout button, so the company doesn't have historical data to compare its performance against the red checkout button. This business question can't be solved using analytics. It needs testing.

So, the product manager sets up a controlled experiment to test the hypothesis. He creates a test webpage to expose part of the website traffic to the red checkout button and the other part to the blue checkout button. Then, the manager observes the checkout behavior of users. Now, he has data from the experiment to analyze; he can determine if the blue button really does drive incremental checkout.

Additionally, analytics can only prove a relationship (A$\leftarrow\rightarrow$B), whereas testing can prove causation (A$\rightarrow$B). In our example, suppose the product manager has seen a relationship between average order size and page load time using analytics, such that the higher the load time, the lower the order size. What he still doesn't know is whether order size drives load time or load time drives order size, or whether both are driven by something else. If he really wants to understand the causation, he will need to set up a testing experiment to change load time and see its effect on order size, or vice versa.

In summary, analytics is analysis of past data to get insights and show relationships. Testing is creation of new sample data through controlled experiments to derive insights and prove a causal relationship.

GROWTH HACKING TO DRIVE CONSUMER GROWTH

What is growth hacking? It is a process within an organization that has the singular focus of driving scalable growth of a growth metric. Facebook used growth hacking to grow from 45 million consumers to 1 billion consumers, and Twitter used it to expand its customer base 10 times. LinkedIn, Quora, and PayPal are other companies that have adopted and continue to use this strategy. Simple mantras of growth hacking have been to make the product market itself rather than be constrained by a marketing budget.

Most organizations look simultaneously at multiple metrics—revenue, customer retention, and many other such strategic priorities. In contrast, many technology start-up companies are now creating a SWAT growth hacking team that focuses on a single metric—like number of customers. Chapter 8 explains the 3 Key Questions framework that lays out a method for a company to identify drivers of growth once such a metric is identified and agreed upon.

To achieve their goals, growth hacking teams operate as a start-up within an organization. They are lean, with a small number of experts who are working together creatively on a small budget and making decisions quickly. A team typically consists of product development, product management, design, analytics, and marketing expertise in an effort to identify and implement what drives a chosen growth metric to increase exponentially. A key tenet is that this growth is scalable and not a one-time spurt. It is made possible with a lot of experimentation, speedy learning, continuous iteration from those learnings, and frequent implementations to learn more, all powered by creative analytics.

The result is a comprehensive acceleration toward that growth by combining the input of all areas into a convergent approach. A growth hacking team would use a "pull" strategy to attract consumers. That is, it will include an experience with the product to drive engagement by understanding user motivations and behavior and provide immediate value to engage customers. This approach is distinct from the traditional modular approach of a marketing department reaching out to engage customers after the product team builds a version of the product. Analytics is a powerful tool in identifying these patterns in the customer behavior data and to continually verify the impact of change in the product.

With Twitter,[4] analysis of the behavior of its existing user base showed that if new users followed at least ten people on Twitter using a simple sign-on process, they were more likely to stay. Thus, Twitter's strategy was to then develop a feature to introduce a new user to a list of top ten people to follow. Further features were added to help new users be followed back. This dramatically increased the odds of that user returning, and the user retention went up significantly. At Facebook, an early hack was to extend Facebook outside of Facebook by allowing users to embed their Facebook widgets like badges and profiles on their own websites and blogs. This gained Facebook an incredible amount of visibility through the Internet, resulting in millions of sign ups. Existing users had been given the facility to propagate their Facebook membership via their own portals!

Growth hacking isn't formulaic, and that is its strength. These are solutions created custom to the organization, its goals, and its products. It asks for incredible buy-in from organizational leadership, as well as team members who transcend the boundaries of their skills.

BEYOND THE HYPE

Big Data is the elephant in the room that we must address. In fact, it is often not very relevant in the context of analytics, although people seem to use the terms interchangeably. Here is why.

What Is Big Data?

Big Data is often explained using three Vs, where a very high Volume of data with lot of Variety is flowing at a high Velocity. The three Vs create issues of storage and visualization. Data analysis has traditionally dealt with structured data. The complexity of variety in Big Data is fed by an expansion of structured data (that can be stored in columns and rows) and an explosion of unstructured data (pictures, text, movies). Traditional business intelligence systems are well set up to handle structured data, but unstructured data can be an issue. A large volume of data has existed for a long time, but it is the addition of the other two Vs that is making traditional business intelligence (BI) systems unstable in the face of Big Data. Big Data is a business intelligence issue, not an analytics issue. Big Data is hard to store and render, and thus requires special tools and technology (thus the Big Data hype). But once the monster of data structuring is done as part of business intelligence, analytics can be done on that data just the same.

When done right, analytics starts with identifying a subset of Big Data to intelligently narrow down the scope using hypotheses—just like Holmes and the treasure in the Pacific Ocean.

So, Big Data is NOT synonymous with analytics, and we will NOT talk about Big Data in this book. We will talk about how smarter decisions can be made using the data to which you have access.

IN CONCLUSION

We can't imagine taking the Christopher Columbus approach to find gold, yet we have seen many businesses go after data with exactly this explorer mentality, flounder with the massive amount of information, squander large amounts of time and resources, and come up with nothing of real business value.

Efficient managers and analysts, on the other hand, can use the guided Sherlock Holmes data-driven approach to direct their efforts as they search for answers that are relevant to the problems at hand. Not surprisingly, these managers and analysts find gold nuggets and drive dollars that impact the organization.

In the next chapter we will delve deeper into some of the analytics methodologies we just touched upon.

IN A NUTSHELL

- Analytics = Data science + Decision science.
- Analytics is not rocket science; any business professional keen on leveraging data for better decision making can do it.
- Analytics is not reporting.
- Analytics is not constrained by Big Data challenges. (When done right, analytics always deals with subsets of data.)

THREE

Top Seven Analytics Methodologies

THIS CHAPTER WILL TALK ABOUT:

The top seven commonly used analytics methodologies.

When to use which methodology.

Typical use cases of analytics methodologies applied to marketing, as well as product and customer service operations.

You are the owner of Gable Wines. The small winery is doing well. Along with producing and selling wine, you host weddings at your beautiful vineyards. With $1 million in annual revenues from your wedding business, you are looking to increase the flow of business. You now spend a small marketing budget of $27,000 on a variety of promotional vehicles, mainly search engines and online wedding portals, but you aren't confident that you're getting the most impact from this approach. Which marketing vehicles are delivering the best leads and sales?

This is a straightforward challenge for business analytics—marketing channel optimization. All you need to do is analyze the results from each promotion vehicle you have invested in, compare the results with the cost, and see which delivered the most conversions at the lowest price to determine the most efficient lead generators.

You start by asking some exploratory questions. What channels are generating good leads? How much should we invest in each of these sources? Should the marketing mix be changed to get better returns?

Your goal is to identify the business questions: Where do good leads come from? How do we get more of these good leads? The next step is to come up with hypotheses on what the answers to these questions could be. Then, we will do an analysis to determine the optimal solution.

Every business has situations like that of Gable Wines—probably multiple situations. These are ideal situations for applying simple data analytics. It doesn't have to be time consuming or costly, and it certainly isn't rocket science. In Chapter 5, we will get into what could be considered borderline rocket science or magic—predictive analytics. You can be the judge then.

THE SEVEN MOST COMMONLY USED ANALYTICS METHODOLOGIES

You can use analytics any time you are facing a management decision that involves data. There is only a short list of analytics methodologies

EXHIBIT 3-1. Seven Most Common Analytics Methodologies (Top 4 are the Most Commonly Used)

METHODOLOGY	DESCRIPTION	APPLICATION
Aggregate Analysis	Used to describe a population or a segment or to compare two segments.	Descriptive analysis, profiling, campaign analysis, winner-loser analysis.
Correlation Analysis	Looks for the relationship between two or more things with the prospect of being able to explain or drive one with other.	Pre and post, test-control, drivers, dashboard.
Trends Analysis	Aggregate or correlation analysis over time, that is, trends over a period of time.	Trends of sales, revenues, breaks in trend and segments or drivers over a period of time.
Sizing/Estimation	Structured approach to make a near-accurate guesstimate in the absence of historical data.	Business case with limited internal data or one that is dependent on external data and assumptions.
Predictive Analytics/Time Series	Looks at both current and historical data to make predictions about future events.	Drivers of conversion or consumer engagement, forecasting.
Segmentation	Groups customers or products into meaningful segments, usually to enable better targeting for the purpose of driving higher value through customization.	Grouping customers or products for targeting and customization.
Customer Life Cycle	Looks at the different stages of the purchase process to determine what stage a group of customers is at and decide how to move them up to the next stage in the purchase process.	Customer progress stages from consideration through purchase to use, sales funnel.

to solve common business problems. The specific business question you are wrestling with will dictate which methodology you adopt. Below we'll introduce the common analysis methodologies and the contexts of their uses. The top seven are shown in Exhibit 3-1; the first four are the most commonly used.

Aggregate Analysis

Aggregate analysis is the simplest and most commonly used analytics methodology. It is also the first step in most other methodologies. It is used to describe a population or a segment or to compare two segments. A population is a collection of things or people you want to understand. It could be customers or prospects. It could be products, such as items produced in a given month or sold in a particular category on your website.

At Gable Wines, you are also looking to understand who is booking wedding events in order to customize your communication. You look at bookings in the last three years, say 300 customers, and do aggregate analysis on age, gender, and location. Analysis reveals 85 percent of them are women, with a mean age of 33, and that 60 percent of them are in Oregon.

You can now use this insight to not only set the tone of your communication but also to target your marketing effort in Oregon. Where can you find women in their thirties? Are there certain stores that cater to that demographic? What publications do they read or follow? Do they eat in certain restaurants? Can you advertise at those locations?

In addition to describing a population, aggregate analysis is also used for comparing segments.

Another business problem you are trying to address is to increase conversion of people filing the online form for wedding reservations. You can compare testing results from the use of the two forms—short form and standard form—and see which gets better conversion.

In summary, aggregate analysis can be used to answer descriptive or comparative questions for your business, such as:

- Who are my customers?
- How are my customers different in one geographical region versus another?
- Do younger people access our digital product through tablets more than older people?
- What worked and what didn't work in the last marketing campaign?

Correlation

Correlation looks for the relationship between two or more things with the prospect of being able to explain or drive one with the other.

> *When looking for good leads at Gable Wines, you take inquiry form submission as your proxy for good leads. Then, you narrow down your initial hypotheses to the four most plausible ones:*
>
> - *Certain wine guides and Google-paid searches produce better leads.*
> - *Mobile users are better leads.*
> - *People seeing the pricing page result in bad leads.*
> - *Certain locations produce better leads, such as the local Oregon area.*
>
> *You would use correlation analysis on each of these hypotheses—conversion by traffic sources, mobile versus not mobile, people seeing pricing pages versus those who do not, and location. With this analysis, you are able to quickly disprove two of the hypotheses, leaving two to explore further—that different traffic sources indeed have different conversion and that geography is a big factor as well.*

Exhibit 3-2 is an example of what the conversion data and correlation analysis for the conversion across various sources looks like.

EXHIBIT 3-2. Conversion Data and Correlation Analysis

SOURCE/MEDIUM	LEAD FORM CONVERSION RATE (IN PERCENTAGES)
Google/organic	4
Google/cost per click	4
Bing/cost per click	1
(direct)/(none)	2
myportlandwedding.com/	5
facebook.com/referral	0
Bing/organic	4
Yahoo/organic	5
stinnocentwine.com/refer	4
wineryweddingguide.com/	10
weddingwire.com/referral	11
eolaamityhills.com/refer	0
apps.facebook.com/refer	0
vibranttable.com/referral	8
google.com/referral	7
others-long tail	3
Average	**3**

By reallocating the budget from bad lead sources to good lead sources, you can drive an incremental gain. First, cut investment on weak lead producers—pay per click on Bing, Facebook page, and certain wine guides. Second, increase spending on the three specific vehicles that were efficient high producers of good leads: Google pay per click and certain wedding guides. Through this simple correlation analysis, you find a 12 percent ($120,000) incremental revenue for Gable Wines with the same $27,000 marketing budget. Of course,

*note that every channel saturates and conversion rates will start to
drop after a certain limit.*

In our experience, a similar data analysis would take two hours using
existing data, a small price for a big benefit, and can be done in Excel
by a nonanalyst who understands the context of the business. No rocket
science, just good solid business analytics that any professional can
do. We will go into complete detail on how to do this in Chapter 4.

In summary, correlation is used to answer business questions like:

- Why is last quarter's revenue below expectation (by finding the
  segments that correlate with revenue gap)?
- Why is the foot traffic down for the Verizon store in Manhattan
  (by finding correlators of foot traffic)?

Trends Analysis

Trends analysis is aggregate or correlation analysis over time, that
is, analysis of trends over a period of time. It most often is used to examine sales performance or revenue growth over time. The goal is to
identify breaks in the trend and pinpoint the impacted segments and
drivers over that period of time. It is used for questions like:

- Has our customer base been shifting to a younger demographic
  (by trending age over time)?
- Why is growth trending down (by looking at growth over time
  and breaking it down by different segments to find correlators
  where the growth is slowing down)?
- Why are sales of the iPhone 5 slowing down (by looking at
  iPhone 5 sales over last few months and identifying internal and
  external correlators to sales)?

Sizing and Estimation

Sizing and estimation is a structured approach to making a near-
accurate guesstimate in the absence of historical data. It is technically

not an analytics methodology, as it does not use historical data. But since it uses a structured approach based on assumptions and limited external and internal data points and is widely used in business to drive decisions, we are covering it as part of analytics. It is typically used to make a business case for going into a new market, to understand the potential marketable universe for a product yet to be launched, and to quickly size up the impact of a decision or change. It is used to answer questions like:

- How many networking routers are sold in the United States yearly, and what percentage of those are sold to consumers?
- How many wedding gowns are sold in Los Angeles annually, and what percentage of that market can we capture?

Predictive Analytics

Predictive analytics looks at both current and historical data to make predictions about future events. FICO scores and weather forecasts are common examples of predictive analytics. Predictive analytics exploits fundamental correlations between a metric of interest at a certain future time and other correlated metrics at a current or historical time. By observing the current and historical correlators, the future state of a metric can be predicted with some accuracy.

Time series is a special application of predictive analytics that doesn't use a different correlator, but rather a metric's own value at previous times, over a period of time. This kind of correlation is called autocorrelation, or relationship with self.

Questions addressed by predictive analytics look very similar to correlation analysis. Examples include:

- What are the drivers of customer churn?
- What drives customer engagement?
- Why is conversion going down, and what is driving it?
- What environmental factors lead to autoimmune conditions in humans?

Yes, even disease diagnostics can have an application for predictive analytics. Often, predictive analytics gets quite complex and that is where it begins to border on rocket science. In Chapter 5, we will look at predictive analytics in more detail. There, too, we will direct readers who want to pursue it even further to other resources and training.

Segmentation

Segmentation is an analytics methodology that groups customers or products into meaningful segments, usually to enable better targeting for the purpose of driving higher value through customization. Those in the same group are more similar to each other and different from those in another group.

Looking at your customer base as current customer and prospect is a simple segmentation. You can segment them further based on products they own—like apparel shoppers and book shoppers, for a company like Amazon. As you can imagine, there are many ways of slicing the pie, and that is determined by why you are segmenting. There are simple segmentation methods, such as RFM (recency, frequency, monetary), product versioning, and demographics. In marketing, RFM is one of the most common techniques of segmentation. In its standard form, these three variables at three levels each—low, medium, high—divide the population into 27 segments.

Here's another segmentation example using product versioning. If you were running a marketing campaign to sell the just-released version 9.0 of your consumer software, then the consumer base can be segmented as prospects, trial downloaders, and version 1.0 users to version 8.0 users, to see who are the best adopters. You may even be surprised to find that version skippers (like those who are on version 6 or 7) have highest adoption versus those using version 8.0.

Segmentation can also be done using a more advanced statistical technique called clustering, which has the capability of considering many variables and offers clusters or segments that are more homogenous internally and more distinct from one segment to another.

You know you need segmentation when your goal is to answer customization questions like:

- How do we customize our offering (to whom do we offer which product)?
- How do we customize incentives (to whom do we offer $10 off and to whom do we offer $50 off)?
- What does our product portfolio look like (more profitable product SKUs versus the rest)?

Customer Life Cycle (CLC) Analysis

Customer Life Cycle (CLC) analysis looks at the different stages of the purchase process to determine what stage a group of customers is at and to decide how to move them up to the next stage.

Cohort analysis is a special type of CLC analysis in which customers are analyzed relative to their start date or active date. For example, the July cohort may need 15 days to habituate to your product, but the December cohort may need 30 days. Sales funnel analysis is another application of CLC. CLC answers questions like, "What is our sales conversion funnel?" That is, of the people who show up as leads, how many qualify, how many become opportunities, how many try the product, and how many become customers? CLC can also answer other questions like:

- How do customers progress through our products?
- How does an Apple customer navigate Apple products? Perhaps some come from using iTunes, then buy through iCloud around the 90-day mark, and then perhaps buy an iPhone about a year later.

CLC is often done in conjunction with segmentation. As you can imagine, Apple's customers acquired through iTunes may have a different CLC than those acquired through enterprise Mac.

Now that you have learned about the top methodologies, test your knowledge using Exhibit 3-3.

EXHIBIT 3-3. Choose the Appropriate Methodology

Which methodology or group of methodologies will you choose for solving these questions? Answers are in the notes at the end of the book.[1]

1. *Why has conversion dropped postlaunch of a product?*
2. *How many elementary schools exist in New York State?*
3. *Determine if and why revenue growth for "Toys and All" has slowed down over the last few weeks?*
4. *Can you tell me which offer worked best in the last marketing campaign?*
5. *Are our London office employees younger than our Singapore office employees?*
6. *What are the time cycles for our customers to go from hearing about us to downloading the free game and then paying for the premium features?*
7. *Of our one million customers, to which 200K should I send the next marketing campaign to get the best ROI?*
8. *What are the different use cases for which our customer is using our printers? What does it mean for us?*

APPLICATIONS OF METHODOLOGIES

Let's look at some common applications of these methodologies to business problems in functions like marketing, product, and customer service.

If You Are in Marketing

Consider a breadth of industries: financial services, consumer goods, ecommerce, automobiles, technology, media, and so on. A CMO broadly expects three key outcomes for business initiatives.

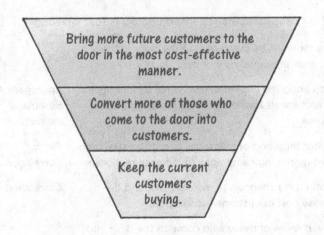

In essence, the CMO seeks a wide and targeted top of the funnel, with higher conversion at every stage. This will achieve maximum revenue at optimal ROI. Data can support an optimized funnel through questions like the following, all of which are represented by Gable Wines.

- To whom and where do I market?
- How much do I spend on each channel?
- What drives response and conversion?
- Who best responds to what message, offer, and product?
- What drives churn?

While this may seem like a compelling case for predictive analytics to some, we think a CMO can realize a better ROI using simple business analytics techniques to arrive at insightful and informed decisions. Exhibit 3-4 provides a sample of how it can be done with very simple analytics methodologies (the specific analytic methodologies are in italics).

If You Are in Product Management or Part of a Business Unit (BU)

The Chief Product Officer (CPO) or head of a BU share similar challenges. Again, he or she can use many of the same techniques and strategies (see Exhibit 3-5).

EXHIBIT 3-4. Business Analytics Methodologies for Marketing

1. Bring more future customers to the door in the most cost-effective manner by:	
• Increasing the marketable universe by identifying new channels based on the existing customer profile.	*Aggregate Analysis Sizing and Estimation*
• Better targeting of messages and offers based on past marketing campaigns to increase response.	*Testing Correlation Analysis*
• Optimizing channels to increase ROI and decrease cost of customer acquisition.	*Correlation Analysis*
2. Convert more of those who come to the door into customers by:	
• Identifying conversion drivers. Do certain fulfillment options, user experiences, review options, cart options, payment options, offers and promotions drive incremental conversion?	*Testing Correlation Analysis*
3. Keep the current customers buying by:	
• Segmenting the base to drive engagement.	*Simple Segmentation-RFM*
• Launching an engagement campaign, customized by segments, to stimulate buying.	
○ Understanding engagement drivers (like certain offers, discounts, bundling, loyalty memberships and such) for each of the customer segments.	*Correlation Analysis*
○ Understand campaign effectiveness—what resonates with customers and what doesn't.	*Testing Aggregate Analysis Correlation Analysis*
○ Understanding drivers of churn—identifying factors that make customers leave your business.	*Correlation Analysis*

If You Are in Customer Service Operations

Similarly, the Head of Customer Service Operations can also leverage analytics to solve key business problems (see Exhibit 3-6).

EXHIBIT 3-5. Business Analytics Methodologies for a CPO or BU Leader

1. Identify new products and features for the various customer segments—understand consumer needs per segment and deliver targeted products:	
• Divide the base to understand differences in needs (based on past product usage, demographic, etc.).	*Simple Segmentation*
• Identify different products and features across multiple segments.	*Testing*
• Prioritize new product ideas or features.	*Sizing and Estimation*
2. Prioritize which product features to include. This can be a determined by understanding the expected business impact.	*Sizing and Estimation*
3. Optimize the customer experience to increase product usage by motivating consumers to take an action, such as buying a product or signing up.	*Testing* *Correlation Analysis*
• Identify friction points that prevent users from using your product successfully.	*Testing* *Correlation Analysis*

EXHIBIT 3-6. Business Analytics Methodologies for Customer Service

1. Optimization of the most precious resource—call routing to agents by customer segment to optimize metrics like FCR (First Call Resolution) and NPS (Net Promoter Score), thereby cost.	*Correlation Analysis* *Simple Segmentation*
2. Satisfactorily address issues of customers who are calling. This in turn means understanding top issues and drivers of resolution.	*Aggregate Analysis* *Correlation Analysis*
3. Who are the most valuable customers? What are the characteristics of each customer segment? What level of assistance does each segment of customer warrant?	*Aggregate Analysis* *Correlation Analysis*
4. Divert customers to self-serve before calling to reduce customer service overhead. This requires understanding the top reasons why customers are calling and creating effective self-service options.	*Correlation Analysis*

IN CONCLUSION

In most cases, simple business analytics can give you a scale of efficiency, instead of waiting for the analytics team to get around to answering your question. The data you will need, most likely, is already at hand; you just have to dig it out and look at it.

In the next chapter we will go through a step-by-step guide of how you can do business analytics on your own to drive smarter decisions and better actions for your business.

IN A NUTSHELL

- Eighty percent of business problems are solved using the four most common analytics methodologies that can be performed using Excel.
- Aggregate analysis is used to describe or compare.
- Correlation analysis is used to find relationships between things and use that to move one with the hope of moving the other.
- Trend analysis is used to analyze trends over time.
- Sizing and estimation is a methodology used to generate accurate estimates from limited internal data.

2

DIVING DEEP

FOUR

B.A.D.I.R.:
Business Analytics
in Five Simple Steps

THIS CHAPTER WILL TALK ABOUT:

The recipe: Five steps to go from Data to Decisions.

How to analyze data using four methodologies that solve
80 percent of business problems.

SmartShoes is an up-and-coming online retailer in the fashion shoe and accessories segment. Its growth has been incredible. A new accessory line, however, was not only missing its targets after a strong start, but also had declining revenue.

Tom, the CEO, stopped to meet with Jeff, the Director of Analytics. Tom says, "I want to see three years of revenue data by department and by country." After a week, Jeff returns to Tom with the information and states, "Revenue for accessories is going down in the U.S." Tom is furious, and asks, "Is this all you could find? This, I already know. I don't have time right now. Let's talk at 7 AM tomorrow."

Jeff was not off to a good start. He may have known what to do with data, but he missed a critical first step: "Getting to the real business question." This is what Tom was *really* asking him to determine. While Jeff showed good intentions in leveraging data and analytics and spent an incredible amount of time and money building complex analytical models, he still did not identify and address the problem.

This chapter introduces the BADIR framework that can take you from Data to Decisions using a set of five lean, streamlined steps that can address 80 percent of business problems using simple, yet powerful, analytics. BADIR stands for **B**usiness question, **A**nalysis plan, **D**ata collection, **I**nsights, and **R**ecommendations (see Exhibit 4-1).

Any manager can follow these five steps to effectively pursue an analytic solution, often without the use of complex methods. Our experience shows that if analytics hasn't delivered results in an organization, it is usually because one or more of the steps has been skipped or not followed in the proper sequence. For example, the business question may not have been clarified, or perhaps stakeholders failed to come up with meaningful hypotheses to explore and test. By the time you finish this chapter, you will be able to solve most business problem requiring analytics by following the framework.

As discussed in Chapter 2, effective analytics is the confluence of data science and decision science. The technical track calls for tech-

EXHIBIT 4-1. BADIR: Five-Steps from Data to Decisions

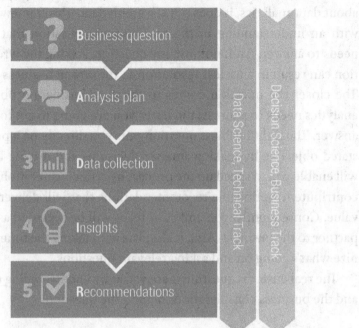

1 ❓ Business question

2 💬 Analysis plan

3 📊 Data collection

4 💡 Insights

5 ☑ Recommendations

Data Science, Technical Track

Decision Science, Business Track

nical skills associated with data science, toward insight. The business track demands softer skills of influencing your audience and understanding the business using decision science, toward impact. The business track is often overlooked by organizations in the thirst for data-based insights. The BADIR framework drives efficacy and results by bringing these two powerful tracks together.

Analytics for impact = Data science + Decision science

STEP 1 • BUSINESS QUESTION

What's in it for you?

- Reduction of iterations.
- Contributions with actionable recommendations.
- Recognition as a partner in the decision-making process.

You may notice right away that even though BADIR is a process about data analytics, it does not start with data. This framework starts with an understanding of the real business question that the data needs to answer. And, not just any question. Asking the wrong question can result in a useless resolution to the wrong business problem. The closer the question comes to the core business problem your analytics needs to address, the faster you are going to get to the right answer. The right business question puts you directly on a path to the stated objective by making smarter decisions and driving impact. It will enable you to speed up the process by reducing iterations and will contribute to actionable recommendations that will deliver business value. Consequently, you and your team will be regarded as a valued partner to the business. And, it all starts with taking the time to recognize what's going on and asking relevant questions.

The real business question is arrived at by understanding the intent and the business considerations behind the question.

Framework to Get from the Stated Objective to the Real Business Question

Start by following the traditional six-question framework: What, Who, Where, When, Why, and How.

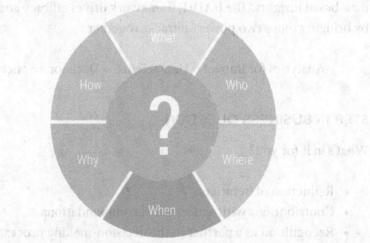

EXHIBIT 4-2. BADIR: Step 1—Business Question

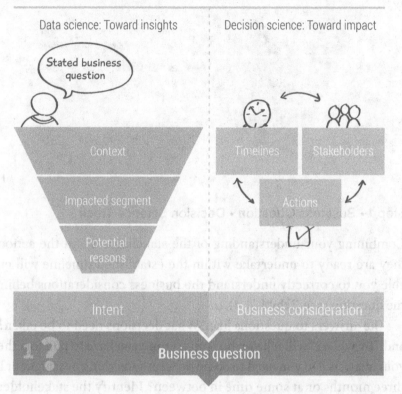

The purpose of asking questions at the beginning is to identify the problem in its context. This is the Sherlock, or detective, approach. The failure to narrow down the issues to the actual problem is similar to searching an entire ocean (of data) to look for gold, which is the Columbus, or explorer, approach. This is where you should be a detective. Ask relevant questions that enable you to understand the present factors, past events, or future strategy driving the request for analytics in the first place (see Exhibit 4-2).

Step 1 • Business Question • Data Science Track

Combining the context, impacted segment, and potential reasons behind the need for analytics will identify the intention behind the request (see Exhibit 4-3).

EXHIBIT 4-3. Ask Questions to Identify Intent

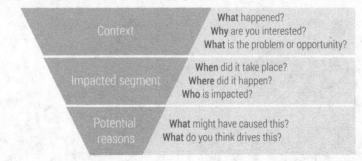

Context	What happened? Why are you interested? What is the problem or opportunity?
Impacted segment	When did it take place? Where did it happen? Who is impacted?
Potential reasons	What might have caused this? What do you think drives this?

Step 1 • Business Question • Decision Science Track

Combining your understanding of the stakeholders and the actions they are ready to undertake within the established timeline will enable you to correctly understand the business considerations behind the question (see Exhibit 4-4).

The answers to questions like "What decisions need to be taken?" and "By when?" will tell you how much time you have to pull together your analysis. Do you need to come up with something overnight or in three months or at some time in between? Identify the stakeholders in this effort by learning, "Who is asking for this analysis?," "Who will be impacted by the analysis and subsequent recommendations?," and "Who will take action on the basis of the analysis?" More important,

EXHIBIT 4-4. Ask Questions to Understand Business Considerations

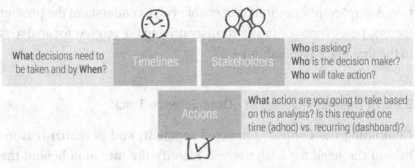

What decisions need to be taken and by When?	Timelines	Stakeholders	Who is asking? Who is the decision maker? Who will take action?
	Actions		What action are you going to take based on this analysis? Is this required one time (adhoc) vs. recurring (dashboard)?

understand what actions your stakeholders are ready to take as a result of this analysis.

If you find that the stakeholders are unable to take action based on the findings, then this analysis doesn't need to be done. If Step 1 is completed properly, eight out of ten requests for data and insights will be filtered out, because the information may prove "nice to know" rather than answer a critical question that would drive the business forward.

Merging the technical and business tracks by combining intent with business considerations would help refine the real business question so you can better target your analysis. Doing this up front will save time, increase relevancy, and efficiently use resources, thereby reducing cost and effort.

Simply put, the more and better questions you ask, the better your results will be. Some words of caution are warranted when working through Step 1 to get to the business question (see Exhibit 4-5).

Pets & Pets is an online pet resource company in the United Kingdom. It has a reputation for not only providing a comprehensive selection of pet products at competitive prices, but also serving as a trusted source of information about pets and pet products. Over the

EXHIBIT 4-5. Steps to Avoid in Finding the Business Question

✗ DO NOT . . .

. . . try to propose a solution to the problem at this stage.
It would preempt discovery of valuable information about your business that you may unearth with a thorough investigation.

. . . ask leading questions.
They will only result in biased answers or no answers at all. Such faulty analysis could, in turn, skew the insights and recommendations you offer.

years, it has captured extensive information about its online visitors. Britney, Chief Product Officer (CPO), asked Alex, Director of Analytics, for online sales conversion data by country, product, and feature for the last 10 years.

Because Alex realizes this will result in a sea of data across the life of Pets & Pets, he first asks relevant questions to understand why Britney wants this information. Alex learns that while he was on vacation, a new feature was tested in the online sales flow for dog leashes to increase conversion. However, the feature actually resulted in a drop in sales conversion. Although only 1 percent of UK traffic was affected, the losses were close to $600,000 per month.

Alex also learned the new feature had many bugs and that there had been some friction over the design. Britney was under great pressure from the CEO. She would need to decide between rolling back the test and giving up the new feature or making adjustments to immediately improve conversion. The former wouldn't be ideal, as Britney's team had worked on this high-visibility project for over two months. She was tending toward the latter choice, but wanted to know what adjustments would be necessary to correct the conversion dip.

Britney was meeting the CEO in two days to debrief. To complete this investigation, Alex narrowed the real business question to: "What are the reasons for conversion drop after the dog leash online checkout feature was launched in the UK?" and "What actions can Product Development, Product Management, and Quality Assurance team take to address the bleeding?"

Notice how different the clarified business question is from Britney's original question (see Exhibit 4-6). In arriving at the business question, Alex also discovered the driver behind this request, the various business considerations, the stakeholders, and the timeline. If he had not arrived at this question, he would have found himself in the same shoes as Jeff at SmartShoes, wasting time and resources to return a data ocean back to Britney, who would wonder why Alex was not able to read her mind.

EXHIBIT 4-6. Pets & Pets: Clarifying the Business Question

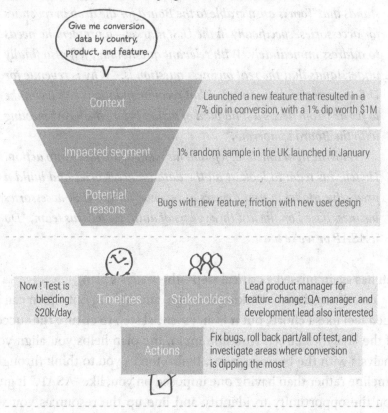

Give me conversion data by country, product, and feature.

Context — Launched a new feature that resulted in a 7% dip in conversion, with a 1% dip worth $1M

Impacted segment — 1% random sample in the UK launched in January

Potential reasons — Bugs with new feature; friction with new user design

Timelines — Now! Test is bleeding $20k/day

Stakeholders — Lead product manager for feature change; QA manager and development lead also interested

Actions — Fix bugs, roll back part/all of test, and investigate areas where conversion is dipping the most

What are the reasons for the conversion drop after the dog leash online checkout feature was launched in the UK? What actions can QA, PD, and PM take to address the bleeding?

STEP 2 · ANALYSIS PLAN

What's in it for you?

- Alignment with key stakeholders.
- Scope management.
- Assignment of proper resources with agreed-upon timelines.
- Delivery in scope and time.
- Line of sight to impact.

Back at SmartShoes, Tom has calmed down. Jeff now understands that Tom is answerable to the Board for the drop in revenues for accessories, specifically in the U.S. market—a problem he needs to address immediately. With relevant questioning, Jeff also finally understands that the real business question is, "Why is revenue for U.S. accessories decreasing? What recommendations can we make to fix it?" Tom needs a solid plan of action before the 9 AM meeting with the Board tomorrow.

With the tight timeline, Jeff and his team again jump into action. He tells his team to look at all the data on accessories and build a predictive model to find drivers of revenue for the U.S. accessories business based on the last three years of data. He tells his team, "Do it ASAP or we're toast."

Jeff has again missed a critical step—the analysis plan.

Yes, sitting down, thinking through, and writing out a plan can indeed feel like a chore, but it is an essential step to ensure the success of the analytics effort. At a minimum, the plan helps you align your analysis with the business need. It also forces you to think through a timeline rather than having one imposed on you, like "ASAP." It gives you the opportunity to identify and line up the resources you will need for the various tasks involved. Finally, it gets you visibility, agreement, and buy-in; this can prove crucial to avoid arguments down the road. (And, you can rest assured, arguments will arise.)

Step 2 • Analysis Plan • Data Science Track

The analysis plan has five building blocks: Analysis Goals, Hypotheses, Methodology, Data Specification, and Project Plan (see Exhibit 4-7).

Step 2 • *Analysis Plan* • *Data Science Track* • **Analysis Goals**

Start by creating a SMART (Specific, Measurable, Attainable, Relevant, and Time bound) analysis goal to answer the business question

EXHIBIT4-7. BADIR: Step 2—Analysis Plan

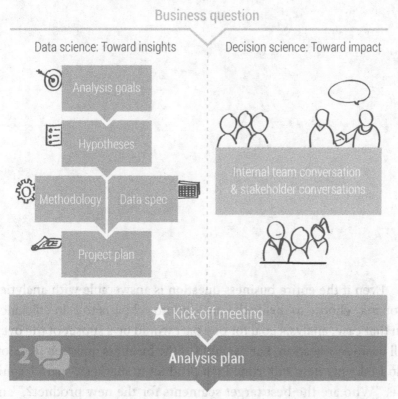

or its subparts as identified in Step 1 (see Exhibit 4-8). It would lay out what you can answer directly with the data you have.

If the business question is, "How would we grow our $100M business to $300M in three years," it is a really major question. To solve that, many aspects of the business need to converge, including strategy, competitive landscape analysis, internal process audit, technology audit, testing, market research, voice of customer, and so on, in addition to analytics. Since analytics can provide solutions to only part of the business question, it needs to be narrowed down to an analysis goal that is agreed to by the stakeholders at a kick-off meeting.

EXHIBIT 4-8. Building Blocks of Analysis Plan: Analysis Goal

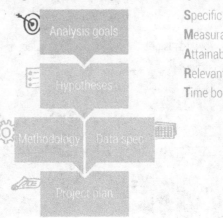

Specific
Measurable
Attainable
Relevant
Time bound

Even if the entire business question is answerable with analytics, you may choose to divide the project into subparts to gain efficiency. In that case, analysis goal for one part would be a subset of the overall business question. For example, if the business question is, "How do I take my new subprime loan product to market?," part 1 could be, "Who are the best target segments for the new product?," and part 2 could be, "Which marketing channels should be used—email, direct mail, phone, inbound—and with what frequency, to avoid unsubscribes?"

> *At Pets & Pets, as Alex and his team prepared the analysis plan, they noted:*
> - *Business question: What are the reasons for the conversion drop after the dog leash online checkout feature was launched in the UK? What actions can QA, PD, and PM take to address the bleeding?*
> - *Analysis goal: Determine drivers of conversion, and segments where conversion in the test population is lower than in the control group.*

Step 2 • Analysis Plan • Data Science Track • Hypotheses

Before determining which data should be collected, come up with hypotheses and criteria to prove or disprove each hypothesis (see Exhibit 4-9). A hypothesis is an informed guess as to what is causing the issue you are trying to address with your data analysis. It describes a possible answer, such as a driver or a reason behind the business question.

A hypothesis usually takes the form of:

$A \rightarrow B$ (A is causing B, and B is part of the business question.)

People often think that hypotheses come from data, but that is not true. Hypotheses are best generated through a brainstorming session with all the key stakeholders based on what they think may be driving the situation. The objective is to come up with multiple possible hypotheses. At this stage, no hypothesis should be shot down, even the seemingly far-fetched or ridiculous ones. You will not have to chase all of them down; rather, you will prioritize all the hypotheses you have collected, ranking them on how plausible or testable they are and their likely impact.

EXHIBIT 4-9. Building Blocks of Analysis Plan: Hypotheses

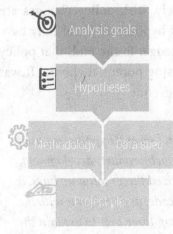

Two separate meetings are recommended:

1. The first should generate the hypotheses.
2. The second should prioritize them.

The best source for generating hypotheses are the people closest to the business, often product managers, marketing managers, and customer service or salespeople who have asked the question or are the people who would actually take action based on the insights.

The prioritization meeting can have a smaller set of people, often more senior stakeholders. They should first agree on criteria for prioritization, such as potential impact or how easy it is to get the data, and then vote on what each one of them thinks are the best bets. A 100 points mechanism works well for prioritization. In this approach, each stakeholder has 100 points to place against the hypotheses. Then, the hypotheses are prioritized based on the total points each has received.

The Aryng team performed an analytics consulting project for a financial services client that wanted to reduce churn. During the hypotheses brainstorm meeting, someone proposed that a change in risk policies may have disqualified potential buyers, thereby causing churn. Without that hypothesis, no one would have looked into such an obscure technical policy more closely. Risk policy changes are often not stored in a database, and this hypothesis could only have been arrived at through business knowledge. In the end, that policy turned out to be the main culprit in losing potential clients. It was easily adjusted to significantly increase revenue.

Alex and his team at Pets & Pets found several hypotheses based on the brainstorming meeting with the web product, development, and marketing teams. They then prioritized three: software bugs, a problem with the untested IE6 browser code, and problems with the new Chrome browser. These were the top three bets to explain the conversion drop in the UK feature launch.

EXHIBIT 4-10. Building Blocks of Analysis Plan: Methodology

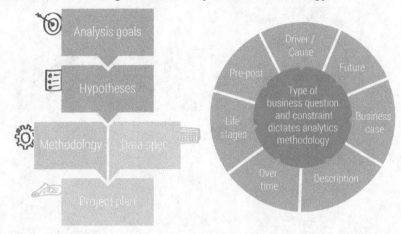

Step 2 • *Analysis Plan* • *Data Science Track* • **Methodology**

The type of business question will dictate the analysis methodology or approach that you will choose (see Exhibit 4-10). As discussed in Chapter 3, there are seven commonly used analytics methodologies, of which aggregate analysis, correlation analysis, trend analysis, and sizing and estimation are most frequently employed.

> *Alex and his team at Pets & Pets identified correlation analysis as appropriate for this project, since they needed to find events that correlated to conversion to explain the drop.*

Step 2 • *Analysis Plan* • *Data Science Track* • **Data Specification**

Based on the hypotheses, the criteria to prove or disprove, and the chosen methodology, collect the necessary data for analysis (see Exhibit 4-11). Two things should be noted at this point:

- Only relevant data that is useful to prove or disprove a hypothesis should be collected.
- Data specifications should be written before you go into data collection.

EXHIBIT 4-11. Building Blocks of Analysis Plan: Data Specifications

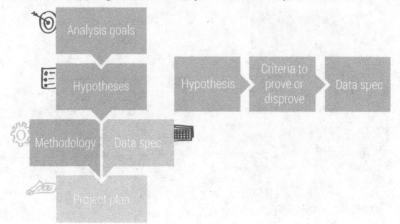

Data collection only begins once the complete analysis plan is agreed upon by the key stakeholders.

The data required for each hypothesis is first identified and then fed into one master data specification, or data spec. As you write the data specification, determine the level of granularity that will be relevant for this analysis—granularity in terms of time, geography, event, or segment. For example, suppose you are pulling sales data. Do you need that at weekly grain, monthly grain, or yearly grain? Depending on the aggregation level you want and the level of the raw data you pull, you may have to aggregate it accordingly. As you do so, make sure it is tied to a unique ID. If you have determined granularity at monthly grain, then the Month_ID becomes your unique ID, to which all the different data elements from your hypotheses are tied—like bugs, incompatible browser, etc.

In the Pets & Pets example, they needed data at the level of transaction attempt, as they needed to understand why certain transaction attempts resulted in conversion while others did not (see Exhibit 4-12). Exhibit 4-13 shows their data specification.

Based on the first hypothesis that focused on bugs, the Pets & Pets team identified that they needed conversion data about buggy and nonbuggy sessions separated into test and control results to prove or disprove that hypothesis. Similarly, they identified the exact data they needed for each of the other two hypotheses.

EXHIBIT 4-12. Pets & Pets Example: Hypotheses and Data Required

Hypothesis	Criteria to prove or disprove	Data required
Bugs in new feature are causing conversion dip	# bugs as % of attempted transactions after conversion dip is higher than before dip	# bugs by test vs. control; conversion for each
IE6 browser feature is not optimized for user experience	Conversion of one browser postconversion dip is trending lower than historical; large enough volumes	IE6 conversion for test vs. control; overlap with above
Possible issues with Chrome	Conversion on Chrome lower in test vs. control	Conversion by browser in test and control

EXHIBIT 4-13. Pets & Pets: Data Specification

All transactional test data postlaunch with this granularity

Variable name	Definition
Txn_atmpt_id	Transaction attempt ID
Bug_Flag	Yes / No flag for whether the transaction was buggy
Browser_Type	Browser used for the transaction
Test_Flag	Test / Control flag
Conversion_Flag	1 / 0 flag to denote conversion or not

Step 2 • Analysis Plan • Data Science Track • **Project Plan**

The project plan ties all the building blocks together and is formulated only after there is a clear understanding of the analysis plan outlined above (see Exhibit 4-14).

The key elements to include in a project plan are:

- **Resources**: What people, budget, hardware, software, other IT resources, other company resources, and outside resources, if any, might you need for this project?
- **RASCI:** Who is **R**esponsible for driving this project, who is **A**ccountable, who plays a **S**upportive role, who needs to be **C**onsulted, and who needs to be **I**nformed. These roles are critical and should be defined up front so people are not stepping on each other's toes or pointing fingers later on. Companies use variations of this model, such as DACI, RACI and ARCI, which have the same elements. We find value in including the support role as well, as this could involve an entire department, such as IT or Project Management.
- **Timeline and milestones:** A timeline, including milestones and appropriate check-in points with stakeholders, ensures visibility

EXHIBIT 4-14. Building Blocks of Analysis Plan: Project Plan

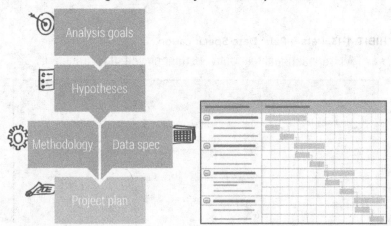

and clarity about when each person will perform his or her role and when key decisions need to be made. For every project, big or small, we recommend a minimum of three milestones: kick-off, initial check-in with findings, and final presentation.

- **Risks:** It is very valuable at this stage to identify all potential risks. For example, the longer the project, the greater the risks associated with missing resources or unexpected hurdles. Having a plan B and even a plan C helps when plan A goes amok and the timeline cannot be compromised.

- **Phasing:** Breaking deliverables into smaller phases gives you means to quickly deliver the first set of actionable insights, while also ensuring you are on the right track. For example, the top five hypotheses can make up phase 1 and the next five hypotheses can be part of phase 2 once the phase 1 results are back. The execution team can then work on insights from phase 1, while phase 2 is in progress.

- **Prioritization:** Finally, you need to ensure that this project is appropriately prioritized for all those who are contributing so that the timeline can be met. Ongoing projects may have to be reprioritized to accommodate this new project. This will need to be addressed appropriately with the respective stakeholders.

Step 2 • Analysis Plan • Decision Science Track

You'll notice that all the building blocks of the analysis plan involve internal team conversations and stakeholder conversations to generate their respective outcomes—from aligning on the analysis goal to hypothesizing to signing off on the project plan. When building your analysis plan, make sure to keep both your internal team and your stakeholders in the loop. Discuss roles, responsibilities, resources, and previous reports that can be leveraged with your internal team. With stakeholders, discuss your analysis plan, with special emphasis on getting alignment on goal, methodology, prioritized hypotheses, and the timeline. The culmination of the analysis plan is a formal kick-off meeting—highly recommended. At this meeting, make sure to get stakeholders to sign off on the analysis plan and get commitment from those who will be doing the work. An analytical plan is not a solution, but rather a clear path to one that is visible to all involved parties.

Alex, from Pets & Pets, used the information from his first meeting with Britney and the subsequent brainstorming sessions with other stakeholders to lay out a plan. This plan gave Alex the information he needed to proceed efficiently, come up with some hypotheses about what the problem might be, identify the appropriate methodology (correlation analysis, in this case), and pull together a project plan. As a final step, he consulted with Britney on the plan, which she tweaked slightly. With confidence in the plan, Britney met with the CEO the next day. At that meeting, she offered the proposed analysis plan rather than a solution to the problem. Alex had clearly established that his team would need a week to get to the core of the issue and come back with recommendations, which Britney and the CEO were agreeable to. With the plan nailed down, they were on the way to getting the answers.

STEP 3 • DATA COLLECTION

Collecting data is Step 3 in the framework (see Exhibit 4-15). Often, this is where people want to start their data analysis effort, but before you can look at data, you need to understand the problem and have an agreed-upon analysis plan so you can strategize your data collection effort.

To speed up the process, Jeff skipped the analysis plan step. Then, to further save time, his team skipped the data cleansing and validation steps. The team failed to think through what data was needed or where to get it. As a result, his team struggled to collect all the data and had to work all night.

EXHIBIT 4-15. BADIR: Step 3—Data Collection

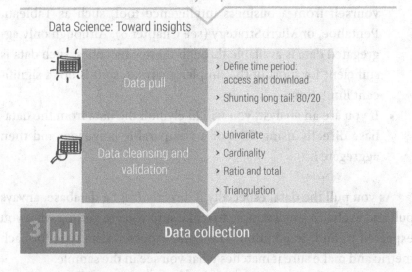

Step 3 • Data Collection • Data Science Track

Remember, GIGO (garbage in, garbage out). The quality of the insights and the value of the recommendations from your analysis depend on the quality of the data you start out with. Data collection, followed by data cleansing and validation, are all therefore important.

Let us talk about the two phases in data collection and quick tips to avoid the most common errors.

1. **Data pull:** Collect the data as per the data specification.
2. **Data cleansing and validation:** Clean the data to make it usable, and validate the data to make sure it is accurate.

Data Pull

Collect the data per the data specification in the analysis plan, which is based on the analysis goal, hypotheses, and chosen methodology. Depending on which side of the business you are sitting on, that process may vary.

- If you are a business professional, have an analyst pull the data for you based on the specification or, better still, pull the data yourself from a business intelligence tool, such as Tableau, Pentahoe, or MicroStrategy (see Chapter 6). Although only aggregated data is available through these data cubes, such data is sufficient for most of the simpler analyses, so it is not a significant limitation.
- If you are an analyst, you will likely pull the data from the database directly using SQL or a comparable language, and then aggregate it.

As you pull the data, especially if directly from a database, always pull and eyeball a small sample to make sure you are getting what you expected to find. In addition, know the expected data type for each metric and make sure it matches what you see in the sample.

Common sources of data errors. The first common source of data errors is multiple sources. You may be pulling data from an application like a CRM system, a web analytic tool, a production environment, a database, or machine data. You may end up with similar data points from different data sources. For that reason and to ensure the consistency of the data used in your analysis, make a point to know the source of every piece of your data (see Exhibit 4-16).

You may find that not every data source defines the data in the same way or in the way you define it. Different sources, for example,

EXHIBIT 4-16. Data Collection Guidelines

TIPS	COMMON ERRORS
• Data should be tied to a unique ID. • Test SQL with small sample of data before pulling a large amount of data. • Match data collected with the expected data type for each metric.	• Historical data with overwritten or misclassified columns. • Data partially appended sometime in history but represented as complete historical data. • Multiple sources, similar data.

may define sales or conversions in different ways, and this might make a difference in your data analysis.

During Aryng's consulting engagement with a Fortune 500 financial services organization, we discovered that the conversion for a particular product was overreported for this very reason. This particular product was being sold to merchants with the promise of much higher conversion than other checkout options in the market. In the end, however, this claim was not true. The conversion for this product was similar to other comparable products in the market. The culprit behind the misreporting was different definitions by the different sources for starts and completes of conversion of this product. There was a huge backlash from merchants when the misreporting was finally disclosed.

The second most common reason for data errors is historical overwriting of data, where the content of the column no longer matches the description. Both these issues require data cleansing, validation, and reconciliation, which admittedly are time-consuming activities. Using data markers like triangulation to spot data issues, however, will speed up the process.

Data Cleansing and Validation

Validate your data as you go about collecting it. Start with a sanity check of a small data sample and compare it with what you expected. Pay attention to null values (data that does not exist in the particular database) and the cardinality (the number of distinct values for that column) of the data. Is it what you were expecting to find? For example, often in self-reported data, like a job title, customers may choose "other" as an option or they may not fill it in at all. Although an answer of "other" is not a null value, if the information is not filled in, it may be stored as null or blank. So checking the cardinality will help you spot issues where "other" as well as a "blank" is being reported as "null" (see Exhibit 4-17).

Similarly, check that the data type matches your expectation. And, most important, triangulate your data by looking at some key

EXHIBIT 4-17. Data Collection: Tips to Validate Data

- Check for null versus cardinality.
- Ensure data type matches your expectations.
- Do a sanity sample check by eyeballing 50 odd rows.
- Triangulate by checking the sum total to see that revenues and key metrics match with other reports.
- Do quick univariate analysis and watch for a large proportion of null, zero, invalid or same values, and values classified as "other."

metrics from the data set you have in hand and matching it to some other distinctly different source. For example, you may have collected revenue data for your company's Japan division to understand its portfolio. One of the easiest ways to validate the data would be matching the Japan revenue from your data set to key published reports from Japan. If they don't match, you know your data has problems. Most of the time, different sources or different definitions are the main culprits.

Alex from Pets & Pets had finished his plan, presented it to his manager, and got buy-in. The team then went about efficiently collecting only the necessary data based on the data specification from the analysis plan, which took very little time to pull as well as validate. They didn't have to work an all-nighter. Instead, they are making plans for an enjoyable weekend.

STEP 4 · INSIGHTS

What's in it for you?

- Structured approach saves time.
- Right methodology delivers relevant insights.
- It leads to impact and actionability.

For an overview of how to derive insights, see Exhibit 4-18.

EXHIBIT 4-18. BADIR: Step 4—Derive Insights

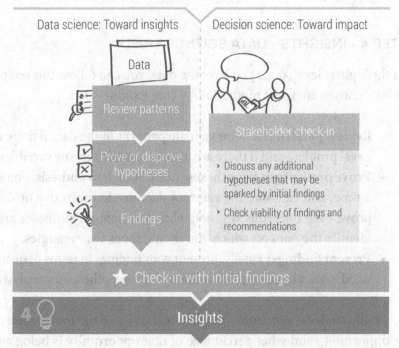

Without a structured approach and having skipped key steps, Jeff's team at SmartShoes is scrambling to get any insights from the model it built. As a result, it is a logistic regression model that the team members hope will bring out the drivers of revenue. After what amounted to an all-night forced march, they arrived with three possible drivers of the revenue shortfall. One was based on incorrect data, as they had skipped the data validation step. The other was so obvious that the only possible response was, "Duh, this is news?" However, one driver, based on correlation analysis, was mildly interesting.

Tom, who had been hoping for a miracle that would relieve the pressure he was under, was sorely disappointed. Not only was this model far too complex to understand or to explain to the Board, but his team did not come back with a single recommendation on how to address the revenue problem for the accessory business. Tom *asked Jeff to come back with recommendations tomorrow. Now he really fears for his job and starts calling headhunters.*

STEP 4 · INSIGHTS · DATA SCIENCE TRACK

At the highest level, once you have the data, you can follow this recipe for any chosen analytics methodology (see Exhibit 4-19).

- **Review patterns**: It helps validate patterns in the data if there is a real problem and if there are unusual patterns in key variables.
- **Prove or disprove hypotheses**: Look at each hypothesis, one at a time, and examine the relevant data needed to prove or disprove each one. This will help eliminate some hypotheses and identify the ones on which you should focus your energies.
- **Present findings**: Finally, present your findings in terms of quantified impact to guide prioritization of the hypotheses for analysis.

In any analysis, remember to call out the size of the total problem or opportunity and what percentage of that opportunity is being addressed by the key drivers that you have identified.

EXHIBIT 4-19. Insights from Data Collected

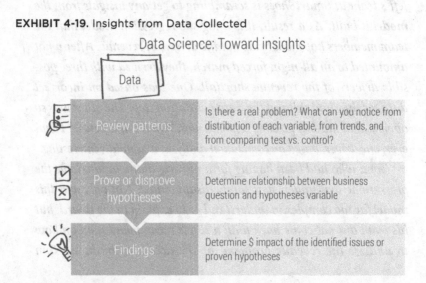

Data Science: Toward insights

Data

| Review patterns | Is there a real problem? What can you notice from distribution of each variable, from trends, and from comparing test vs. control? |

| Prove or disprove hypotheses | Determine relationship between business question and hypotheses variable |

| Findings | Determine $ impact of the identified issues or proven hypotheses |

Of the seven analytic methodologies defined in Chapter 3, the four most commonly used are aggregate analysis, correlation analysis, trend analysis, and sizing and estimation. Let's look at each in turn.

Aggregate Analysis

Aggregate analysis short circuits the action to prove or disprove hypotheses, as it is used most frequently when doing descriptive analysis, such as profiling, or comparative analysis, such as campaign analysis and winner-loser analysis (see Exhibit 4-20).

- **Review pattern:** When using this methodology, look at relevant metrics and slice the data by different segments. A common use case is to determine which marketing campaign was successful and in which demographic segment. Approach this problem by looking at segments with the best and worst bounce rate, unsubscribe rates, open rate, and click-through rate (CTR).

EXHIBIT 4-20. Aggregate Analysis

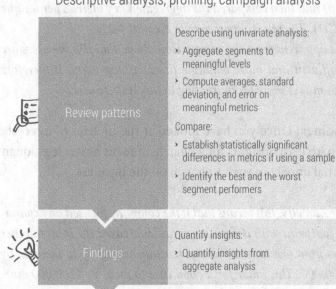

Descriptive analysis, profiling, campaign analysis

Review patterns

Describe using univariate analysis:
- Aggregate segments to meaningful levels
- Compute averages, standard deviation, and error on meaningful metrics

Compare:
- Establish statistically significant differences in metrics if using a sample
- Identify the best and the worst segment performers

Findings

Quantify insights:
- Quantify insights from aggregate analysis

EXHIBIT 4-21. Zameify: Aggregate Analysis

	iPhone	Desktop
Age (average)	25 years	32 years
Income (average)	$125,000	$95,000
# Visits / Unique user	2.4	1.3
$ Spend / Unique user	$42	$15

The marketing team from Zameify, a gaming company, wants to determine if iPhone players are more valuable than desktop players in terms of demographics and engagement. This would directly influence the company's marketing strategy and targeting. In their analysis plan, the marketing and analytics team members identified the key attributes they want to look at for this analysis—age, income, number of visits on iPhone apps in a day vs. website visits, and dollars spent. They had collected these data elements for desktop and iPhone users throughout the life of the product. To review the pattern, they segmented sessions by most common access (iPhone vs. desktop) and then compared the aggregated key metrics per unique user (UU). The results are shown in Exhibit 4-21.

It is apparent from the comparison above that iPhone users are more affluent and more valuable than desktop users. It therefore perhaps makes sense for marketing to target these users.

- **Findings**: Once you have looked at the metrics of interest and come up with crisp insights for a change in focus or strategy, quantify the potential impact of such a change on the business.

For Zameify, this means that if the company focused on expanding its footprint with iPhone users and increased the total number of users from one to two million, revenue was likely to increase by $42,000,000. This made for a good case to focus its $100,000 marketing spend on iPhone users.

Correlation Analysis

In correlation analysis, you look at variables that correlate with something that the business is trying to impact. This analysis methodology is used most frequently to solve business problems related to understanding drivers of the business or an event (see Exhibit 4-22).

At Pets & Pets, the problem was an unexplained drop in conversion after a feature launch. Alex and his team identified the analysis goal, outlined three hypotheses, identified the criteria needed to prove or disprove each, and outlined the data required. Once the team collected the data, the members started by following the three actions for the correlation analysis to try to prove or disprove each of the three hypotheses.

EXHIBIT 4-22. Correlation Analysis

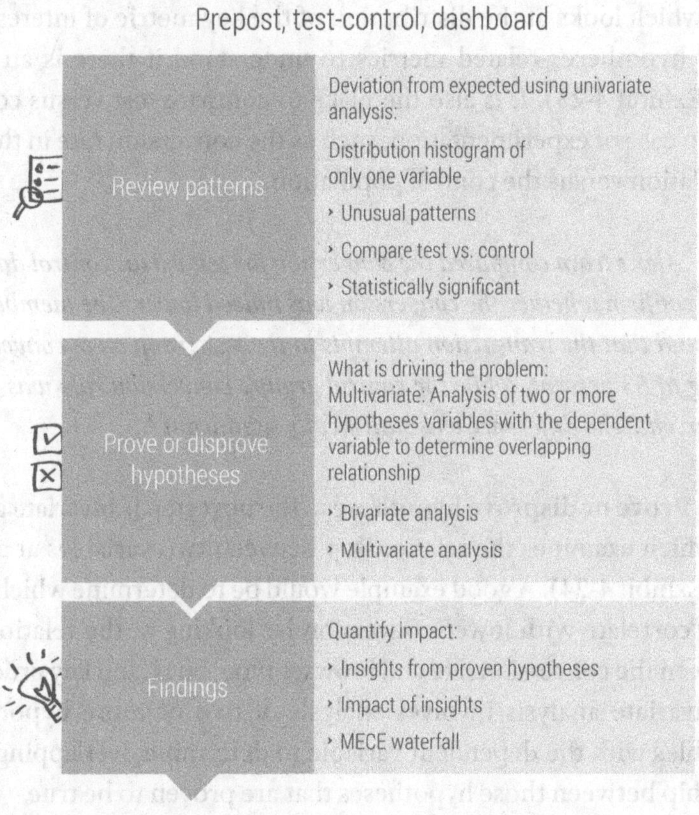

Prepost, test-control, dashboard

Review patterns

Deviation from expected using univariate analysis:

Distribution histogram of only one variable

› Unusual patterns
› Compare test vs. control
› Statistically significant

Prove or disprove hypotheses

What is driving the problem: Multivariate: Analysis of two or more hypotheses variables with the dependent variable to determine overlapping relationship

› Bivariate analysis
› Multivariate analysis

Findings

Quantify impact:
› Insights from proven hypotheses
› Impact of insights
› MECE waterfall

EXHIBIT 4-23. Pets & Pets: Univariate Analysis

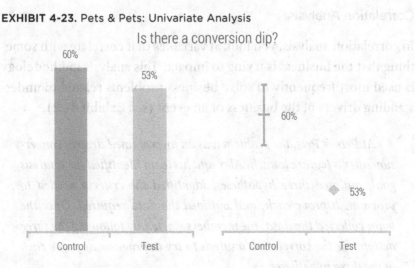

Is there a conversion dip?

- **Review patterns:** Correlation analysis starts with univariate analysis, which looks at the distribution of the key metric of interest and other hypotheses-related metrics to understand if there is an issue (see Exhibit 4-23). It is also the place to compare test versus control data in case of experimentation, such as the conversion rate in the test population versus the control population.

> *Alex's team compared the conversion for test versus control data to confirm whether the conversion was indeed lower. The members found that the transaction attempts in the test group were converting at 53 percent, while the control group's conversion rate was 60 percent. The difference was statistically significant.[1]*

- **Prove or disprove hypotheses:** The next step is bivariate analysis, which examines the relationship between two variables at a time (see Exhibit 4-24). A good example would be to determine which variables correlate with lower conversion by looking at the relationship between the conversion rate and browser type, bugs, and key products. Multivariate analysis involves analysis of two or more hypotheses variables with the dependent variable to determine overlapping relationship between those hypotheses that are proven to be true.

EXHIBIT 4-24. Pets & Pets: Bivariate Analysis

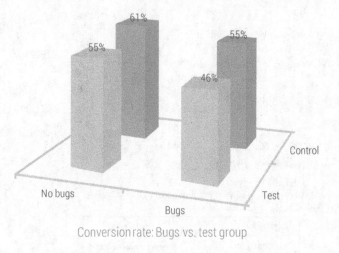

Hypothesis #1: Bugs are causing conversion dip

Conversion rate: Bugs vs. test group

| Bugs | 84% |
| No bugs | 90% |

Test:Control conversion ratio

Alex's team takes the first hypothesis that bugs are causing a conversion drop. The members look at the ratio of conversion rate for the test population compared to the control population for buggy versus not-buggy transactions. The result showed that the conversion for buggy sessions had a lower test-to-control population conversion ratio. This indicates that the programming bugs were definitely one of the factors bringing down conversion. Similarly, they looked at all the other hypotheses proving that the IE6 browser was also causing conversion downturn, while Chrome was not.

Alex's team then does a trivariate analysis to look at the combination of variables that have been proven to impact conversion to determine if the combined effect of both variables has an impact on conversion. Conversion numbers indicated that buggy IE6 sessions had the lowest conversion. The results are shown in Exhibit 4-25.

EXHIBIT 4-25. Pets & Pets: Trivariate Analysis

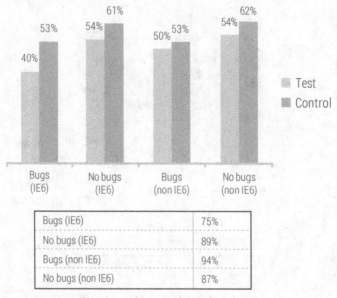

Proven hypotheses: Bugs and IE6 browser correlated with conversion

	Test:Control conversion ratio
Bugs (IE6)	75%
No bugs (IE6)	89%
Bugs (non IE6)	94%
No bugs (non IE6)	87%

- **Finding:** Finally, quantify the impact of the proven hypotheses, that is, of the insights that will drive recommendations (see Exhibit 4-26). Quantifying insights helps build the case for them to be actionable. To do this, rank all of the insights based on their chronology, interdependence, or size. Then, quantify the impact of the first insight (i.e., the one that happens first in a series of events, the one on which all the others depend), or the biggest. Next, quantify the impact of the second after removing the impact of the first, and continue until all the insights have been accounted for.

> Quick Tip: Quantifying any metric into its dollar impact will engage your stakeholders and is a common language that each group can understand. For example, a 1 percent conversion drop results in a $2 million revenue drop.

EXHIBIT 4-26. Pets & Pets: Quantify the Impact

Mutually exclusive and completely exhaustive (MECE)

Proven hypotheses	Test population	Conversion delta	Conversion impact	% impact
Bugs (IE6)	1,502	13%	0.9%	12.7%
No bugs (IE6)	4,275	7%	1.4%	19.4%
Bugs (non IE6)	4,061	3%	0.6%	7.9%
Other	11,557	8%	4.3%	60.0%
Total population	21,394	7%	7%	100%

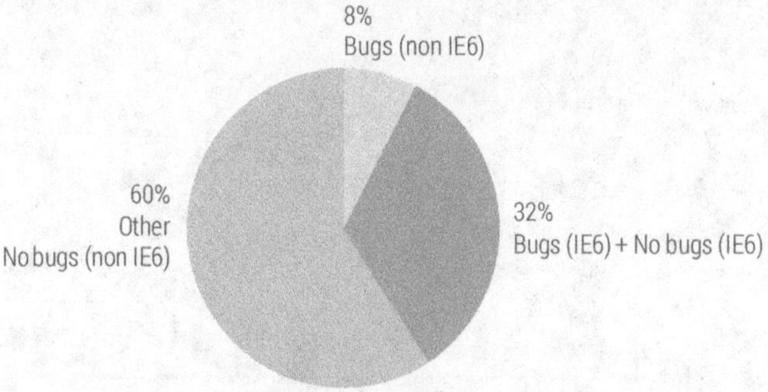

8%
Bugs (non IE6)

60%
Other
No bugs (non IE6)

32%
Bugs (IE6) + No bugs (IE6)

Finally, look at the same impact visually represented in a water-fall for ease of understanding. A table also helps if it ties each proven hypothesis with the percentage of its overall impact so people can understand at a glance which ones are the key drivers (see Exhibit 4-27).

Alex's team found that:

1. *Bugs on IE6 were causing 13 percent of the drop.*
2. *IE6 was causing 20 percent of the drop.*
3. *Other bugs were causing 8 percent of the drop.*
4. *Chrome was not an issue.*
5. *60 percent of the conversion drop was still unexplained.*

EXHIBIT 4-27. Pets & Pets: Waterfall

Insights: IE6 and bugs are the known fallout reasons

Proven hypotheses	Test population	Conversion delta	Conversion impact	% Impact
Bugs (IE6)	1,502	13%	0.9%	12.7%
No bugs (IE6)	4,275	7%	1.4%	19.4%
Bugs (non IE6)	4,061	3%	0.6%	7.9%
Other	11,557	8%	4.3%	60.0%
Total population	21,394	7%	7%	100%

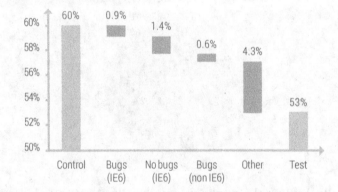

Trend Analysis

Trend analysis is the third most frequently used analytics methodology. It is used to analyze trends in sales and revenues, as well as breaks in trends. It can also be used to analyze segments and drivers over a period of time. The steps in trend analysis are similar to those used in correlation analysis (see Exhibit 4-28). The key difference is that you look at data over a period of time.

EXHIBIT 4-28. Trend Analysis

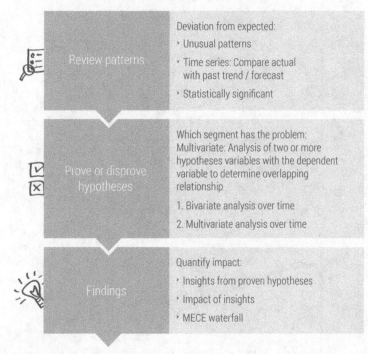

Analyze trends of sales and revenues and identify breaks
in trend and segment/drivers

Review patterns

Deviation from expected:
> Unusual patterns
> Time series: Compare actual
  with past trend / forecast
> Statistically significant

Prove or disprove hypotheses

Which segment has the problem:
Multivariate: Analysis of two or more
hypotheses variables with the dependent
variable to determine overlapping
relationship

1. Bivariate analysis over time
2. Multivariate analysis over time

Findings

Quantify impact:
> Insights from proven hypotheses
> Impact of insights
> MECE waterfall

- **Review patterns:** Look at breaks in trends and patterns over time (see Exhibit 4-29).
- **Prove or disprove hypotheses:** Prove or disprove key hypotheses around those trends by bivariate (see Exhibit 4-30) and trivariate analyses (see Exhibit 4-31). Sometimes trends in key metrics by themselves will not paint a complete picture. In these cases, you need to look at trends in growth rate and similar metrics to tease out breaks in the trend line.
- **Findings:** Quantify the impact of each finding as is done in correlation analysis (see Exhibit 4-32).

(text continues on page 89)

EXHIBIT 4-29. Zameify: Trend Over Time

Plot revenue over time to see breaks from trend and compare with forecast

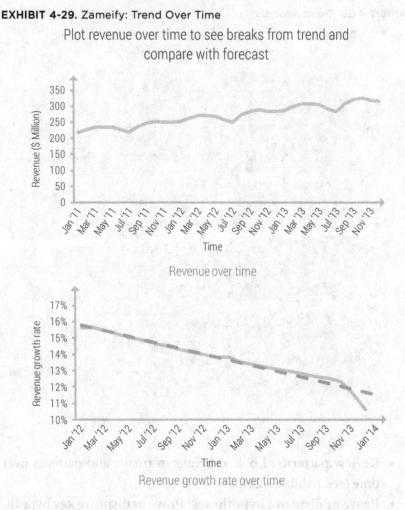

Revenue over time

Revenue growth rate over time

EXHIBIT 4-30. Zameify: Bivariate Over Time

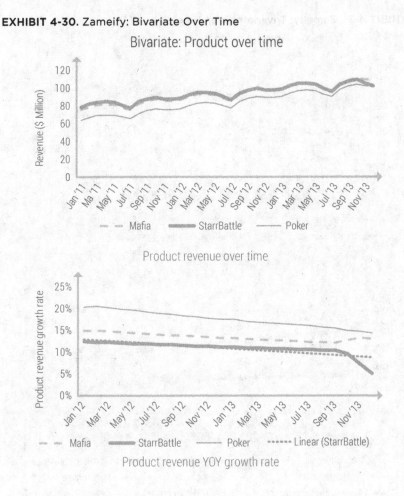

Bivariate: Product over time

Mafia   StarrBattle   Poker

Product revenue over time

Mafia   StarrBattle   Poker   Linear (StarrBattle)

Product revenue YOY growth rate

EXHIBIT 4-31. Zameify: Trivariate Over Time

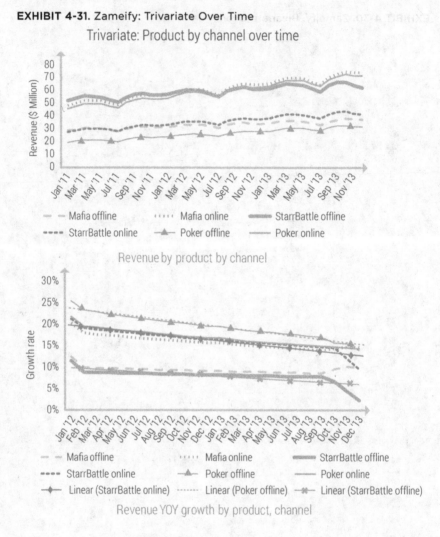

Trivariate: Product by channel over time

Revenue by product by channel

Revenue YOY growth by product, channel

EXHIBIT 4-32. Zameify: Quantify the Impact

Insights: The slowdown is coming from StarrBattle and poker offline segments

Proven hypotheses	Monthly revenue ($)	YOY growth gap	% Impact
StarrBattle offline	61M	5%	52%
StarrBattle online	41M	5%	32%
Poker offline	31M	3%	17%
Total population	314M	1.9%	

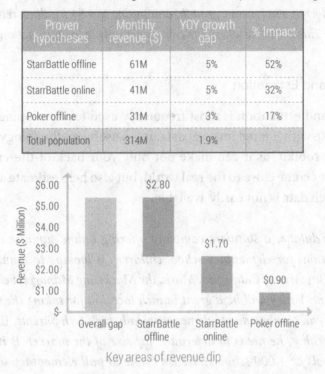

Key areas of revenue dip

Zameify, the gaming company we introduced earlier, is looking to determine the cause of a slowdown in revenue growth. The company started with hypotheses of possible slowdown coming from specific products or channels. Investigators discovered that although revenue was still growing, revenue growth was clearly declining.

So, Zameify looked at revenue split by products over time and determined that the StarrBattle growth rate had been declining in recent months, while Mafia was growing. Similarly, in looking at the revenue split by channels over time, Zameify determined that offline revenue growth is found to be tanking.

Using trivariate analysis, combining product and channel, Zameify finds that the growth rate for StarrBattle was declining both online and offline. Additionally, poker offline wasn't doing too well.

Zameify then proceeded to quantify the impact of each of the find-
ings. The company found that StarrBattle contributed to 84 percent of
the decrease in revenue growth, amounting to a $4.5 million revenue
gap. This is clearly where the company needs to focus its actions.

Sizing and Estimation

Sizing and estimation is most frequently used for developing a business case with limited internal data. It is a useful methodology to have
in your toolkit, as it can make not only your back-of-the-envelope
estimates come close to the real world, but also help estimate anything
for which data is not easily available.

Edulane, a software company offering online summer camp
solutions for elementary school children, is looking to launch in
the Bay Area of California. Mark, the Marketing Manager, believes
Silicon Valley will be a great launch location for taking the sum-
mer camp online due to demographically high-tech parents. Before
launching, he needs to determine the size of the market. Is it 100
schools or 1,000 schools? He isn't able to pull elementary school
numbers specific to the Bay Area with available open-source data.
So, he quickly estimates the number of elementary schools in the
area (see Exhibit 4-33).

There are five parts to address any sizing problem:

1. **Stratification:** Dice the problem into smaller pieces and identify segments that behave differently in relation to what you are
   estimating.

   Mark thinks that the density of elementary schools would
   be different in suburban parts of the Bay Area as compared
   to urban parts. So, he breaks the problem into suburban and
   urban segments, which will likely have different assumptions
   and computations.

EXHIBIT 4-33. Eudulane: Sizing/Estimation

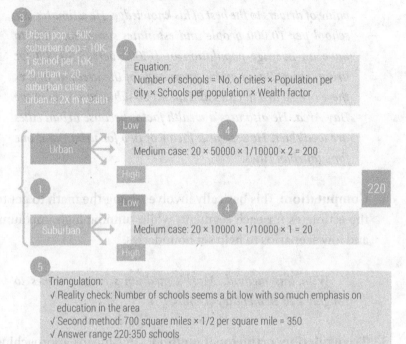

3

Urban pop = 50K,
suburban pop = 10K,
1 school per 10K,
20 urban + 20
suburban cities,
urban is 2X in wealth

2

Equation:
Number of schools = No. of cities × Population per
city × Schools per population × Wealth factor

Urban

Low

4

Medium case: 20 × 50000 × 1/10000 × 2 = 200

High

1

220

Suburban

Low

4

Medium case: 20 × 10000 × 1/10000 × 1 = 20

High

5

Triangulation:
√ Reality check: Number of schools seems a bit low with so much emphasis on
  education in the area
√ Second method: 700 square miles × 1/2 per square mile = 350
√ Answer range 220-350 schools

2. **Correlations and drivers:** Determine what metrics and factors could have any influence on the metric you are sizing. Write it up as an equation.

> *Mark determines that cities, population, and wealth factors could have an influence on the number of elementary schools. Thus his equation is:*
>
> *Number of schools = Number of cities × Population per city × Schools per population × Wealth factor*

3. **Assumptions:** What do we know about the various factors that make up the equation? The assumptions could be different for each segment identified in the stratification.

For each segment, Mark makes assumptions about the value of drivers to the best of his knowledge. He estimates one school per 10,000 people and estimates suburban cities to have an average population of 10,000 versus 50,000 for urban cities. Based on his knowledge of the area, he figures there are 20 urban cities and about 20 suburban cities in the Bay Area. He also uses a wealth factor because urban cities are wealthier. He assigns a factor of two for urban and one for suburban cities.

4. **Computation:** This basically involves doing the math to get to the estimates for each segment, while running high, medium, and low scenarios to help set boundaries.

   With this method, Mark's medium scenario comes to roughly 220 elementary schools.

5. **Triangulation/orthogonal method:** This means approaching the same estimation problem with a very different set of drivers. Triangulation provides a great way to get a reality check on previous assumptions and calculations. For this, you would repeat the first four actions again while choosing a completely different equation to corroborate the results of the first approach. If they don't match up, then you may need to reevaluate your assumptions or come up with yet another approach to triangulate.

   Mark repeats sizing the first four actions using an orthogonal approach with a completely different set of correlators. He considers the total area of the target market area in square miles, making the assumption that there would be one elementary school for every one-half square mile. The result is a total of 350 elementary schools. With this technique, Mark corroborated his first estimate, which was be-

tween 220 and 350 elementary schools in the Bay Area. In
fact, this was a significantly close estimation of the market.

Mark's estimate can be further corroborated by looking up elementary school for the Bay Area in the Yahoo directory, which lists approximately 180 schools by name. Since not all schools would be listed in the directory, Mark's estimate is pretty close.

STEP 4 • INSIGHTS • DECISION SCIENCE TRACK

As the decision science track results in finding insights, it is time to validate these findings with the key stakeholders. This is also a great opportunity to find any additional hypotheses sparked by these findings. Sometimes the data to prove or disprove these additional hypotheses may already be available. If so, it is great to incorporate those into the insights before the final presentation. If the data is not available or is not easy to pull, put these hypotheses in the next phase of the analysis plan and detail them as "next steps" in the presentation to stakeholders so they are clear on the status of the analysis.

At Pets & Pets, Alex and his team had been doing things correctly all along. They found that bugs and IE6 were the main culprits. Alex then turned to validate these findings with the product development team. The engineers were not surprised by Alex's findings, although they were a little sheepish at being found out. They had rushed to launch the UK pilot on a very short timeline. Although they had an inkling that some of the changes might not work well with the IE6 browser, they compromised on optimization and use-case testing for browsers to meet the deadline. Alex then laid out his recommendations to address the issue. The engineering team members were not only supportive, but they also gave him an estimate of time and resources to make these changes, which they promised would get the highest priority as soon as they got a thumbs-up from Britney. With his findings validated, Alex planned to meet with

Britney the next day with actionable recommendations that included
a forecasted timeline to resolve the issue.

STEP 5 · RECOMMENDATIONS

Jeff put together an 80-slide deck for Tom that showed the specif-
ics of the powerful model that laid out the technical details (i.e.,
misclassification, ROC curve, etc.) and showcased the modeling
abilities of his team. After five minutes, Tom stopped the presenta-
tion and asked, "So what should we do differently as a result of this
model?" Jeff did not have an answer to that question, so Tom walked
out in frustration. Jeff was left wondering why Tom was not pleased
with such a complex model that his team had created in record time
by working crazy hours.

Recommendations are the last and most important step of the
BADIR framework. Why? Because solving the problem is the reason
the organization went through this analysis in the first place. If you've
done your analysis well, your recommendations would be actionable
for the organization. This—the recommendation step—is your opportunity to move the stakeholders to action.

You want to achieve three things with your recommendations in
addition to solving the problem (and getting credit for your team, of
course).

First, you want to engage your audience. That means you need to
present a short, concise, and insightful set of recommendations without getting bogged down in details. Without question, you need to
know the details, but keep them to yourself unless asked. Second, you
want to be perceived as an effective business partner, and this will
happen if your recommendations are seen as sound and credible. Third,
you want to drive your audience toward actions that create impact, in
that they solve the business problem.

Let's learn from Gary Klein's *Source of Power: How People Make
Decisions* (MIT Press, 1999). Stakeholders will not take the time to
synthesize your insights. In their quest for the solution, they will grav-

EXHIBIT 4-34. BADIR: Step 5—Recommendations

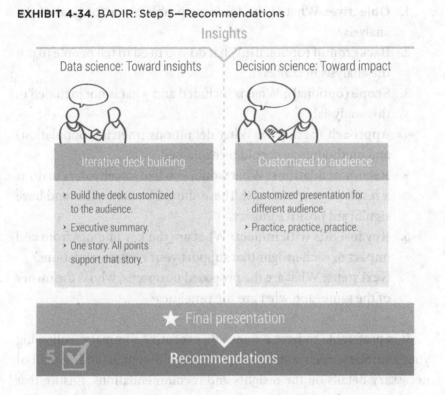

itate toward the first reasonable recommendation, as they have entrusted you with coming up with the best solutions within the business context. It is therefore imperative to present well-researched and accurate recommendations that you can defend (see Exhibit 4-34).

Step 5 • Recommendations • Data Science Track

To be concise, start with an executive summary that should be short, clear, and compelling. Most important, however, it should answer the following key question for audience members, "What's in it for me?" The executive summary should include the following seven components (a few are optional depending on the audience), particularly if the audience has not been involved in the initial discussions leading up to this effort:

1. **Objective:** What is the business problem and/or goal of the analysis?
2. **Background** (optional): What do you need to tell people to put the analysis in context?
3. **Scope** (optional): What is included and what is not included in this analysis?
4. **Approach** (optional): What definitions (metrics, population) and methodology should be explained?
5. **Recommendations:** What would you like stakeholders to do as a result of your findings? These should be actionable and have significant positive impact.
6. **Key insights with impact:** What are the key findings from and impact of each insight that support your recommendations?
7. **Next steps:** What are the proposed next steps, who is the owner of the same, and what are the timelines?

It is preferable to have a one-slide executive summary. Following your summary, each subsequent slide should contain additional but necessary details on the insights and recommendations. Ensure that everything in the deck ties to the story and is built around your key message, with supporting points as necessary. The best decision-making meetings often do not go beyond the first few slides, and almost all the discussions often center on the first slide itself!

Format the slides to a consistent look and feel for ease of consumption. Remember to combine graphics and text. If you are making a longer presentation, use divider slides to transition between topics.

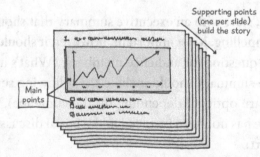

The creation of a slide deck is iterative. We usually make three passes:

1. In the first pass, pile all your findings and tables together and then whittle them down to the key findings and your main message.
2. In the second pass, add the executive summary with key recommendations and findings. You can move detailed slides into an appendix.
3. In the final pass, streamline the flow of the deck and add slides to support the insights in the executive summary. Delete everything else or move other material into an appendix.

Step 5 • Recommendations • Decision Science Track

As you prepare your presentation keep in mind who your audience is and what its members need to know. Create different presentation

decks for different audiences. In addition, pay attention to how the presentation will be delivered—in person or electronically via email and corporate Intranets. If you are giving the presentation before a live audience, give the members time to absorb it, ask questions, and initiate a discussion. A successful presentation should generate a lot of discussion, so encourage it.

Congratulations! You have followed the BADIR approach from start to finish (see Exhibit 4-35).

EXHIBIT 4-35. BADIR: Five Steps from Data to Decisions

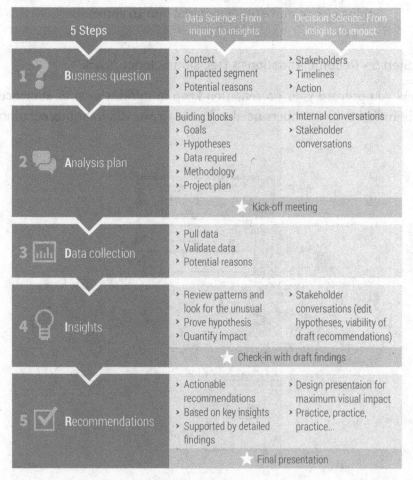

5 Steps	Data Science: From inquiry to insights	Decision Science: From insights to impact
1 ? **B**usiness question	› Context › Impacted segment › Potential reasons	› Stakeholders › Timelines › Action
2 **A**nalysis plan	Buiding blocks › Goals › Hypotheses › Data required › Methodology › Project plan	› Internal conversations › Stakeholder conversations
	★ Kick-off meeting	
3 **D**ata collection	› Pull data › Validate data › Potential reasons	
4 **I**nsights	› Review patterns and look for the unusual › Prove hypothesis › Quantify impact	› Stakeholder conversations (edit hypotheses, viability of draft recommendations)
	★ Check-in with draft findings	
5 ☑ **R**ecommendations	› Actionable recommendations › Based on key insights › Supported by detailed findings	› Design presentaion for maximum visual impact › Practice, practice, practice...
	★ Final presentation	

Alex presented specific recommendations in a four-page deck, starting with the executive summary that called out action items. The recommendations were specific, actionable, and had buy-in from the stakeholders.

1. *Involve product development to fix bugs and diagnose IE6 implementation issues. This would fix $2.9 million of the $7 million impact. Expect to spend five development days for a resource cost of $15,000.*

2. *Conduct hypotheses-driven analysis to explain the rest of the drop in conversion while product development works on fixing above issues.*

Britney was pleased that all was not lost with this test. She had renewed confidence that once these implementation issues were resolved, the new flow would eventually result in higher conversion as expected. Not only was Alex able to have significant impact in the organization, but he was now regarded as a key business partner by Britney and the CEO.

TEST IT

Once you have used the BADIR framework to develop insights, mitigate your risks by testing them out before you do a full launch of a product or an offering. Such testing will validate whether the results you expected based on your analysis can really happen. In other words, is there really a causation? For example, let's say URetailnline's product manager responsible for "high-value customers" discovers that those who sign up for URetailnline Prime (free two-day shipping as part of a yearly subscription) within 10 days of opening a seller account become high-value customers. This is a great insight, which the product manager can then use to incentivize customers to sign up for URetailnline Prime.

However, until he tests it out with a small sample and sees the increased activity, he won't know whether signing up for URetailnline Prime (A) is truly a causation toward high value (B) (i.e., A→B). It could easily be just reverse causation, in which high-value customers are likely to sign up for URetailnline Prime (B→A). If the latter is true, offering an incentive to sign up for Prime may increase Prime sign ups, but it will not increase the number of high-value customers.

For a deeper dive on testing, refer to complete A/B testing training covering the BADIR framework on the Aryng website (aryng.com).

The next chapter dives deeper into more advanced methodology—an overview of predictive analytics.

IN A NUTSHELL

- BADIR is a highly effective Data-to-Decision framework to solve business problems. It is industry nonspecific and simple to adopt.
- To truly move the needle on the business using data and BADIR, follow both the technical track and the business track toward insights and impact.

FIVE

Predictive Analytics, aka Rocket Science

THIS CHAPTER WILL TALK ABOUT:

Overview of predictive analytics.

How to build a predictive model using BADIR.

It was windier than usual late that February evening when Bruce McCauley pulled his silver Honda Accord into the parking lot of his apartment complex in West Santa Cruz, California. His heart was racing. He had planned this for months. His face lit up as he opened a small red box, and the rock on the ring glistened in the dim glow of the street lamp. He and Kate had been together for a little over a year now. With an elaborate proposal planned for early the next morning, he couldn't think of a better place to hide the ring than the glove compartment of his car. The windy evening gave way to a cold and foggy night. As Bruce peered through his bedroom window at the car before going to sleep, he thought about how dreamy it looked outside in the thick fog that engulfed the city that night.

Meanwhile, on the other side of town, Lieutenant Chad Foster, officer of the Third Precinct, Santa Cruz Police Department, was starting his night shift.[1] He turned on the ignition, reached for the police radio, keyed the microphone, and advised the dispatcher that he was "10-8"—in service, ready for duty. After attending to service calls for the evening, he parked in a vacant lot to catch up on paperwork. Then, his radio sounded. The MASC (Mathematical and Simulation Modeling of Crime) system had just generated a crime prediction. An organized criminal activity was about to occur in a parking lot in West Santa Cruz. MASC even pinpointed the hotspot down to a 250-foot radius. "10-4, on my way," he relayed back to dispatch.

With headlights turned off, he covertly scoped the seemingly uninhabited parking lot of the apartment complex. He saw two shadows at a distance approaching a car. The suspects had broken into a silver Honda Accord and were about to make a clean getaway when they were confronted by Lt. Foster. As he placed them both under arrest for auto theft, he recognized one of the perpetrators, a felon he had arrested earlier for burglary. The felon's accomplice was just out of prison and on probation for armed robbery. Lt. Foster recovered two items from their custody—a small red box containing a ring and a 9-mm semiautomatic pistol.

Lt. Foster smiled as he transported the felons back to the precinct. Using the power of good data and predictive analytics, MASC had turned the department from a reactive organization to a proactive one that could prevent crime, often before any damage was done. McCauley and his now fiancée thanked Lt. Foster early the next morning, crediting luck and a good police force, never realizing that predictive analytics was working behind the scenes.

As it turns out, predictive analytics was playing a bigger role in the department than just anticipating crime hotspots. With a 20 percent staff reduction and a 30 percent increase in service calls, the department had to allocate resources more efficiently. Department leaders recognized that they had a significant amount of high-quality, fully validated data, so they began asking key questions about the best way to use that data—questions that could be answered with analytics. These included: "How can we reduce response time?," "How many people are needed per shift?," "What times of the days should the shifts be (a big win for predictive analytics)?," "How can our limited resources be allocated efficiently?," and "How can we allocate the time of the officers when not on call (the time Lt. Foster usually spent filling out paperwork)?"

The analytics initiative quickly paid off. The department credits predictive analytics with over 25 arrests and a 19 percent reduction in

burglaries over the first 19 months of its use. Although the line shifts of officers hadn't changed, analytics gave them areas to focus on, and this resulted in greater efficiency.

Chapter 5 is all about this magical side of analytics—predictive analytics. It is complex, but its impact can be immense. The chapter is divided into two parts. Part 1 is an overview of predictive analytics. It discusses where and how to apply predictive models to drive the biggest business impact and is relevant to all readers. Part 2 discusses how to build a predictive model using the BADIR framework and when to pursue predictive analytics further. This section is for business professionals who anticipate using predictive analytics to solve some of their business challenges in partnership with data scientists.

We don't expect this chapter to turn you into a skilled predictive analytics modeler. But we do hope it will make you sufficiently knowledgeable to consider predictive analytics when addressing business problems and enable you to engage effectively with predictive analytics professionals.

PART 1: PREDICTIVE ANALYTICS AND ITS COMMON APPLICATION

What Is Predictive Analytics?

The past predicts the future. Predictive analytics uses statistical techniques to analyze current and historical facts to make predictions about future events or behavior. It is also used to improve the accuracy of insights gained from business analytics. The most commonly used statistical techniques in predictive analytics are regression and classification. *Regression* models a continuous target (the variable we are trying to predict), typically using linear regression, such as modeling the lifetime value of a customer. *Classification* looks at discrete targets through a decision tree or logistic regression.

Consider this example from an online ecommerce company selling apparel and accessories. The company has cart conversion of 40 percent. That is, of the 100 people who put something in their carts, 40 actually checkout and pay. The product manager is trying to identify drivers of conversion with the prospect of increasing that rate. A test was conducted with different colors of the cart button. Analysis of the test data revealed that the blue cart button has a 2 percent higher conversion rate. This is powerful information, as the manager can now earn incremental revenue with the same number of starting visitors just by using a blue cart button. A similar correlation analysis between three-step checkouts (control) versus two-step checkouts (test) also gave him an understanding of the relative success of these two versions, with the three-step checkout having the higher conversion rate.

As you would imagine, many more variants could lead to a successful conversion. To understand the relative impact of each variant, the manager needs a combined equation that includes all variants in order to explain the resultant conversion. So, the product manager worked with a data scientist to build a predictive model that would enable him to understand the drivers of conversion. In this model, these hypothesized attributes can be analyzed together to understand the predictive correlation between a variant (behavior or event) and conversion. He can then simply pull the lever on one or more predictive variants to influence the resultant conversion (assuming the correlation is also causal).

They find that the top positive predictors are the use of Google Checkout as the primary payment choice, no banner ads during the checkout process, the blue cart button, the three-step checkout process, and a page load time of less than seven seconds. The model predicts a 7 percent incremental conversion with all these changes. Armed with these insights, the product manager can now test and then roll out changes to the checkout process to capture the incremental conversion. So, the use of predictive analytics often delivers higher impact than business analytics alone because a larger number of variants and their interactions are evaluated (Exhibit 5-1).[2]

We encounter predictive analytics frequently in our day-to-day lives, even though we may not recognize it. FICO, the best-known and most widely used credit score model in the United States, uses predictive analytics based on demographic and behavior data that has been col-

EXHIBIT 5-1. Case: Identify the Key Parameters That Drive Conversion of a Website Visitor into a Buyer

ANALYSIS TECHNIQUE	PARAMETER EVALUATED	KEY RESULTS	PROS AND CONS
Business analytics	Red versus blue buttons	Correlation analysis of test data indicates a 2 percent higher conversion with blue checkout button.	[+] Quick and easy. [-] Not exhaustive, so may miss the top parameter that can drive the biggest business outcome.
Predictive analytics	Multiple parameters modeled	Top predictor—use of Google Checkout as the primary payment choice, no banner ads in checkout process, blue checkout button, three-step checkout process, and a page load time less than seven seconds.	[+] Builds on insights from business analytics. [-] Time and resource intensive. [+] Can evaluate hundreds of metrics and thus identify the most important parameters to drive largest business outcomes.

lected as individuals spend money and pay off (or do not pay off) their bills. The FICO score, or more accurately, the model it is based on, enables banks and credit providers to understand the credit worthiness of their customers. That way, these institutions can determine which individuals are high credit risks and can decline to issue credit to those who are less likely to pay back the loan.

Common Business Applications of Predictive Analytics

In addition to the credit industry, marketing and advertising have traditionally used predictive analytics. The goal is often to increase both the marketable universe and the ROI on marketing campaigns. For example, you are selected to receive credit card offers based on the findings of a credit model, such as FICO, and a response model. Based on these findings, the appropriate offer is sent to top credit worthy individuals who are most likely to respond. The question is how do companies know that you are more credit worthy *and* that you are more likely to respond. This is determined by your prior activities and behavior, along with those of other individuals with similar attributes. The Amazon recommendation tool, which suggests the next product you may like based on your purchasing and browsing history, is a great example of an upsell predictive model. The banner advertisement you see when you open your LinkedIn profile is also likely based on a predictive model that selects the most relevant ad to show you—one that your profile indicates carries the highest promise of your clicking on it.

Predictive analytics has also seen wide application in improving the customer experience through retention and churn models, customer service operations, and customer experience optimization models. Churn occurs when customers drop a product or service; it is a common industry concern that is actually quite predictable as customers leave telltale signs before they drop a product. Predictive analytics can detect these signs, proactively identify these customers, and also reactively help reactivate them. For example, calls to your phone company may be routed to a work-at-home customer representative, a domestic customer operations center, or an offshore customer operations based in Brazil. The choice is based on your predicted lifetime value, as well as specific customer experience attributes, such as how comfortable you are talking to a non-native English speaker.

The gaming, entertainment, and mobile industry made widespread use of predictive analytics in product management, where it is used to optimize product and feature launches, improve product adoption and profitability, and increase conversion. Next time you see recommendations for movies on Netflix, know that this is predictive analytics at work. However, if your teenage daughter uses the same Netflix account, you may not always like the conflicting recommendations you see there! Netflix has begun to address this customer issue through a feature release of up to five discrete profiles within each shared account.

Now let's look at some real life examples from our experience show-ing how predictive analytics can be used to drive significant business impact.

Increasing Marketable Universe

A software retailer captures $35 million in new revenue by increasing its marketable universe by a factor of four.

Situation: A well-known software vendor catering to creative professionals was seeking new prospects for its second most popular product, called Product X. Current practice was to market the new version of Product X to users and trial downloaders of earlier versions. The analytical task was to find a new revenue source for this product.

Action: The retailer had a database of 50 million prospects who had downloaded a free version of other products. We saw this as a great opportunity to mine for prospects who might have similar attri-butes to users of this product, although they had not shown any prior interest in Product X. Using logistic regression, we scored each pros-pect with an adoption probability score (to adopt Product X) based on the attributes of past users of Product X. The top 4 million prospects were then sent an offer for the latest version of Product X.

Impact: The model increased the retailer's addressable market by a factor of four and resulted in $35 million in new direct revenue. Ad-ditionally, this prospect set became a source of incremental revenue for all future releases of Product X.

Reducing Product Friction

A payments company captured incremental $18 million in revenues by reducing product friction.

Situation: An online payments company had a low conversion rate for its checkout product. Product managers had previously relied on market research to understand the reasons why consumers were drop-ping off before completing their checkout. Primary market research reported many friction points for consumers, but the organization didn't understand the relative size of each friction point. Additionally, leadership did not have confidence in the self-reported issues by the consumers. This was considered a huge opportunity as a 1 percent conversion improvement promised increased revenues of $10 million.

Action: We used logistic regression to build a conversion model and identified key issues driving the low conversion rate. We also used a decision tree and business logic to determine the most likely reasons and to quantify the impact of each. Then, we partnered with product managers to launch a test based on the top issues found using the model.

Impact: Focusing on just *one* of the drivers of conversion gave the organization $18 million in incremental revenue.

Activating Inactive Customers

A financial services company generates $20 million in revenue by activating inactive customers.

Situation: A financial services company targeting subprime consumers included a significant percentage of customers who had been inactive for more than 12 months. Neither reducing the APR nor offers of increased credit lines had significantly impacted this group.

Action: We used logistic regression to build an attrition model to identify drivers of inactivity. To quantify the significance of pursuing these customers, we also built models for each of the key profit drivers to determine expected profits from each consumer on retention. Finally, for each consumer segment, we developed multiple offer combinations that would still yield profits based on inputs from the above models.

Impact: Identifying and rolling out these offers resulted in reactivating these customers, with an incremental revenue of $20 million.

Product Recommendation Engine

A payments company reduces marketing spend by 70 percent while collecting more than $20 million in incremental profits through a product recommendation engine.

Situation: A payments company had multiple payment products to fit the needs of its customers—the merchants. It was observed that merchants who owned more than one product were more engaged and had wider and deeper product usage that resulted in higher profitability. Because of this, the marketing team decided to offer every product to every merchant through marketing campaigns, but this resulted in confused merchants and high unsubscribes. So, the head of marketing wanted to figure out how to find the Next Best Product (NBP) recommendation for each merchant, thereby optimizing adoption as well as profitability.

Action: We used a multiclass decision tree to identify segments of merchants with higher adoption rates for certain products over others. We then combined the adoption data and historical profits to find the expected incremental profit (EIP) per product per segment. With this recommendation engine, the product with the highest EIP became the next best product recommendation for merchants with similar attributes to those in the particular segment. The model was then scored in the database to be used for outbound and inbound marketing.

Impact: Using the NBP recommendation engine, the marketing team now knew which offer to send to whom, resulting in a 70 percent reduction in marketing spending. Additionally, offering the right products using the NBP score resulted in sixfold increase in conversion and an increase of more than $20 million in profits just from the outbound marketing effort.

Summary

The payments company, the software retailer, the Santa Cruz police, and many others have discovered that predictive analytics results in better targeting of products to specific segments of the market, a wider consumer base, and increased profits.

PART 2: BUILDING A PREDICTIVE MODEL: THEORY AND PRACTICE

This section will be most useful for two groups of readers: business professionals who practice business analytics and data analysts in mature organizations. We will introduce terminology and theory applicable to predictive analytics and model building. Understanding this material will help business professionals engage in easier and informed discussions with their data scientist counterparts. We will then describe how to build a predictive model, concluding this section with additional resources that will help you pursue the subject further.

Terminology

Let's start with variables, predictors, and time windows. We'll use the shopping cart example from the first section to show proper usage.

- **Dependent variable**—A variable that is the object of the particular predictive analysis. It is determined by the business question that the model is designed to solve. Conversion, for example, is a dependent variable.
- **Independent variables**—Unknowns that may have a relationship with the dependent variable and no relationship with each other. These are determined by the hypotheses developed to solve the business question. The blue button and the presence of the banner in the checkout process described in the earlier example are independent variables.
- **Predictors**—Unknowns that have been found to have a relationship with the dependent variable. The terms predictors and independent variables are sometimes used interchangeably.
- **Time window**—There are two time windows of importance as you think about building a model: the observation window and the prediction window (see Exhibit 5-2). The observation window (T_0-T_1) is the period during which you are observing and collecting the independent variables for analysis. The sample which you will use for building the model needs to be qualified by the starting of the observation window, T_0. Take our cart example. If you decided to observe all cart activity for one week, your observation window is one week. The prediction window (T_1-T_2) is the period for which you want to predict the dependent variable. You take the value of the dependent variable as of

EXHIBIT 5-2. Observation and Prediction Windows

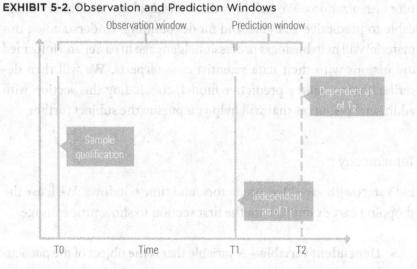

T_2, the end of prediction window. The prediction time window can be long or short depending on how far into the future you want to predict. In general, the longer the prediction window, the higher the error in prediction. However, a shorter prediction window lessens its usefulness to the business, because the business has less time to act before the prediction becomes the present state. You could predict conversion for each session by using 30 minutes as the prediction window. During that time, you would observe whether conversion happens or not.

- **Correlation**—The statistical measure of the linear relationship between two or more random variables, as represented by the correlation coefficient (r) with a value at or between +1 and −1. Predictive modeling exploits the inherent correlation between the dependent variable as of T_2 and independent variables as of T_1. The model's accuracy is greatly increased by finding stronger and more of these underlying correlations, which is why it pays to come up with a good set of hypotheses.

    Remember, all correlations start with the hypotheses that you defined in the very beginning—in step 2 of BADIR. In the cart example, the analysis began with the hypothesis that the blue button correlated to higher conversions. As you find more and more underlying correlations, your model has stronger prediction ability.

- **Misclassification:** One of the ways to evaluate model performance. It is the ratio between the total number of incorrect predictions and the total number of predictions. It is a tradeoff between widening the net to get a greater number of possible results (sensitivity) and tightening the net so you get very specific results (specificity). The lower the misclassification, the better the model. Let's go back to the Santa Cruz police department example. If the police wanted to catch more than just the two car thieves, they would have to open up their model (increase sensitivity and lower specificity), but there's a good chance that they might catch some good guys in the net. If they increase specificity to only catch bad guys, they may miss a few bad guys who don't match those very specific attributes.

Of these two types of misclassification, sensitivity measures the percentage of positives that the model predicts to be positive (true positive, TP), while specificity measures the percentage of negatives that the model predicts to be negative (true negative, TN). The opposite of TP is false negative (FN); the opposite of TN is false positive (FP). Analytically speaking, let's say, a crime model built to detect bad guys catches 11 out of 13 (TP = 11; FN = 2; sensitivity = 11/13), but in the process it also catches 3 out of 16 good guys (TN = 13, FP = 3, specificity = 13/16) (see Exhibit 5-3). If the business cannot afford to not catch the two bad guys, then a modeler might tighten the model parameters to catch more of the bad guys (increase sensitivity), but may end up catching more of the good guys as well (decreasing specificity). Depending on the business objective, sometimes we need to trade in higher specificity to get higher sensitivity, and vice versa. This is a decision a modeler should make with his or her respective business counterpart.

EXHIBIT 5-3. Model Performance

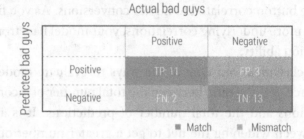

Actual bad guys

		Positive	Negative
Predicted bad guys	Positive	TP: 11	FP: 3
	Negative	FN: 2	TN: 13

■ Match   ■ Mismatch

Common Predictive Techniques

Linear regression, logistic regression, decision trees, k-means clustering, times series forecasting, survival analysis, and neural networks are some of the most commonly using predictive techniques in the business (see Exhibit 5-4).

Of these, the first three are the most frequently used.

- **Linear regression:** A statistical technique that quantifies the relationship between a continuous dependent variable (y) and one or more continuous independent variables $(x_1, x_2 \ldots)$. Its most common application is predicting customer lifetime value (CLV). Say you're predicting the total lifetime revenue from a customer $(y = CLV)$. As you build the model, you may find the top predictors of CLV are the customer's historical annual revenue till date (x_1), yearly income (x_2), etc. Linear regression predicts y as a function of $x_1, x_2 \ldots x_n$. It works by finding a line (hence, the name) though the data that minimizes the squared error (distance) from each point. In a formula, it looks like this:

$$y = a + b_1 x_1 + b_2 x_2 + \ldots + b_n x_n$$

- **Logistic regression:** A special case of regression in which the dependent variable is not continuous. Instead, it is discrete, or categorical, and mostly binary (0/1). It is most commonly used

EXHIBIT 5-4. Common Predictive Techniques and Their Application

TECHNIQUE	DESCRIPTION	APPLICATION
Linear regression	Approach to model linear relationship between scalar dependent variable and one or more independent variables.	Customer lifetime value, cost of acquisition.
Logistic regression	Special case of linear regression where dependent variable is binary in nature.	Churn or attrition model, fraud detection model, and response model.
Decision tree	Type of tree diagram used to determine best classification of population (based on independent variable) to optimize prediction of dependent variable.	Cross-sell product prediction, customer segmentation.
K-means clustering	Segmentation technique to partition population (number of observations) into clusters in which each observation belongs to the cluster with the nearest mean.	Unsupervised customer segmentation, that is, clustering for statistically similar attributes, but not driven by any target variable such as churn or customer lifetime value.
Time series forecasting	Techniques used to forecast future events based on known past values of same event.	Sales over time, forecasting.
Survival analysis	Technique used to predict time to event.	Hitting credit limit, customer tenure.
Neural networks	Generalizations of existing statistical models; black box; hard to understand but more powerful than other techniques.	Fraud detection, response model, and many others.

when there are a number of independent decisions, or discrete actions, like churn and fraud prediction. Let's say we are trying to predict whether a customer will churn or not. In this equation, p represents the probability of churn and y in the equation above is replaced by a log representing the odds of churn occurring, log $(p/(1-p))$. As you build the model, you may find that the top predictors of churn are average time spent on the help pages (x_1), income (x_2), etc. Logistic regression predicts as a function of $x_1, x_2, \ldots x_n$. In a formula, it looks like this:

$$\ln\left(\frac{p}{1-p}\right) = a + b_1x_1 + b_2x_2 + \ldots + b_nx_n$$

- **Decision tree:** Top-down classification structure based on data generated through recursive partitioning, which simply means repeated evaluation and partitioning at each node until the model is able to deliver the desired results. A decision tree is a greedy algorithm that helps identify the most significant predictors quickly. It is the most visual technique lending itself to rule-based scenarios. In our example, a decision tree is used to predict good risk for a financial institution that extends credit to its customer (see Exhibit 5-5). This decision tree outputs the rule that if customers have an income of more than $40,000 without high debt or if customers have an income of less than $40,000 but they are not renters, then they are good risks and credit can be extended to them. Here, the dependent variable is risk (good versus bad) and income, high debt, and renter status are predictors.

EXHIBIT 5-5. Linear Regression

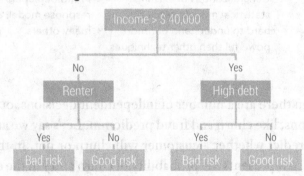

How to Build a Predictive Model

Be it predictive analytics or business analytics, BADIR is relevant to drive decisions using data (see Exhibit 5-6). The specific activities and components used will vary within steps 2 to 5 of BADIR when using predictive analytics as the methodology.

EXHIBIT 5-6. Predictive Modeling Using the Five-Step BADIR Framework

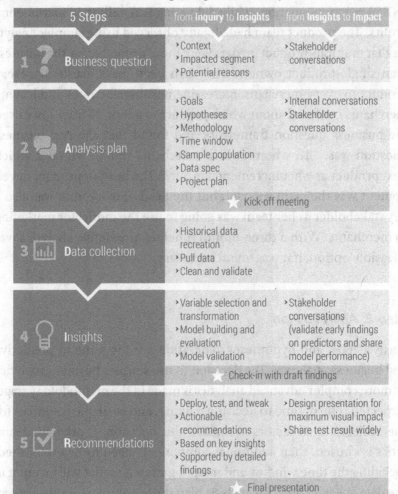

5 Steps	from **Inquiry** to **Insights**	from **Insights** to **Impact**
1 ❓ Business question	› Context › Impacted segment › Potential reasons	› Stakeholder conversations
2 💬 Analysis plan	› Goals › Hypotheses › Methodology › Time window › Sample population › Data spec › Project plan	› Internal conversations › Stakeholder conversations
	⭐ Kick-off meeting	
3 📊 Data collection	› Historical data recreation › Pull data › Clean and validate	
4 💡 Insights	› Variable selection and transformation › Model building and evaluation › Model validation	› Stakeholder conversations (validate early findings on predictors and share model performance)
	⭐ Check-in with draft findings	
5 ☑ Recommendations	› Deploy, test, and tweak › Actionable recommendations › Based on key insights › Supported by detailed findings	› Design presentation for maximum visual impact › Share test result widely
	⭐ Final presentation	

Step 1: Business Question

This step is the same in predictive and business analytics, and it is a critical step that must be taken before determining *which* methodology you will be using to solve the business question. If you are doing analytics properly, you will start with the simpler business analytics methodology described in phase 1 to prove the case for using more advanced techniques like predictive analytics in a subsequent phase.

In Example 4 above, we helped a payments company reduce marketing spend by 70 percent through an optimized Next Best Product (NBP) recommendation, while delivering $20 million in incremental profits. The product team had already observed using simpler analytics that multiple-product owners were more profitable for the business than single-product owners. They had been mass marketing every product to every merchant, increasing unsubscribe rates and leaving merchants confused about which product to adopt. In Step 1, we used the business question framework and found that the real business question was: "To whom (which merchant) should we offer which next product at what incremental profit?" The head of product development was the main sponsor, but the head of marketing was also a key stakeholder as her team was going to use the model for marketing to merchants. With a three-month timeline, predictive analytics was a feasible option, if it was found necessary.

Step 2: Analysis Plan

Analysis goal and hypotheses generation are the same in predictive and business analytics. The decision to use simpler business analytics or more complex advanced analytics is made in the methodology stage. Expected return, time to decision making, and available resources for the project are all factors in making this decision. If predictive analytics is chosen, then additional components need to be established, including the time window and sampling strategies that will be input in the data specification. An analysis plan is not complete until a project plan is laid out and internal and external conversations happen. Then, at a kick-off meeting, stakeholders agree to the plan and contributors agree to pitch in.

For the payments company described above, we narrowed the analysis goal to: "Score the next best product at the individual merchant level by optimizing the merchant experience and increase profits by using past adoptions as an indicator of a positive merchant experience." We generated more than 200 hypotheses based on brainstorming with the stakeholders and chose to include them all in this phase, as predictive analysis was conducive to such input. A significant advantage of predictive analytics over business analytics is the ability to evaluate a large number of hypotheses and do it faster using advanced statistical methods. But remember that data collection will take more time if you have more hypotheses, no matter which methodology you adopt. We decided to use decision tree and logistic regression as the predictive analytics methodologies, as Next Best Product is a discrete outcome. Often, more than one model is built using different techniques to find the best model with the lowest misclassification. We wrote the data specification for the required historical data. To optimize the recommendation engine for both profitability and experience, we devised an innovative heuristic approach to add the profit metric to the probability of adoption of a specific next product. At the kick-off meeting, our clients really valued our approach, as it gave them a single solution that could optimize the customer's experience and increase profits through customer adoption of the next product. Once our clients were on board with the proposed plan, the stakeholders promised their top resources and time to make this project a success. Such buy-in is critical for the implementation and success of any analytics project.

Step 3: Data Collection

In this step, you will find that historical data often needs to be re-created, needing extensive cleaning and validation. Here, two different data sets are needed: one to build the model (training and in-time validation sample) and another to validate it (out-of-time validation sample). The data for the training and in-time validation comes from the same time period. The training sample is used to build the model's logic to predict the target variable, while the validation sample is used to assess the model's performance in being able to predict the target variable. Then, the model is validated on another sample from a different time—called an out-of time validation sample. For example, first using 2012 customer and transactional data for training and in-time validation to predict the next best product model, and then using 2013 data to test this model's performance on data from a different time. So don't be surprised if this step takes 80 percent of your time. For the payments company, it took us approximately six weeks from the analysis plan to pull, clean, and validate the data.

Step 4: Insights

It is at this step that predictive analytics becomes a heavily involved statistical process, including variable selection to choose the top independent variables, model building to identify the equation that connects the independent variables with the dependent variables, and model validation to finalize the equation and the independent variables.

Variable selection is an iterative process in which we transform and treat independent variables to increase predictive power on the dependent variable (see Exhibit 5-7). For the NBP model, one of the independent variables was account creation date. That variable in its original state (as a date) is unusable for model building because it is not a continuous variable nor does it have meaningful discrete values. So, the variable used instead was account age, that is, how long a merchant had been a customer. Then, we calculated the correlation of account age with their NBP. Based on that, further transformation of account age was needed, where square root of the account age had a higher correlation to NBP than any other mathematical transformation. All the 200 plus variables were appropriately transformed just like this variable, and the variables with the highest correlation to NBP were selected.

EXHIBIT 5-7. Variable Selection

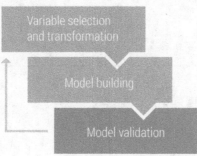

This selected subset of variables are then fit into a model, where the dependent variable is expressed in terms of independent variables in an equation (as in the case of regression) or a tree (as in the case of decision tree).

Model building too is iterative, and often the sequence above needs to be repeated until a model is built that meets the bar with acceptable misclassification and errors, as determined through a business lens. Once a model is built on a training sample, it is validated on an in-time sample to ascertain its stability. Validation on out-of-time samples makes sure the model has not picked up a seasonal or temporary pattern that is unique to the training sample.

Sometimes, to increase the overall prediction accuracy, you may want to build more than one model and combine them (also called an ensemble). As discussed in Chapter 4, the 2006 Netflix Prize was won by an ensemble.[3] Ensemble models may increase prediction accuracy, but they can be harder to explain and operationalize, so this is something critical to consider as you build the model. It is easy to get carried away with predictive analytics, especially when it comes to multiple models. Remember, whatever you do, you will have to explain it to people who aren't as excited or as involved in the analytics as you are. They are looking for answers—your recommendations—in a quick, digestible form that they can use to take informed action.

Once the model is validated, it is a great time to check back with the stakeholders to receive input on the final list of predictors and model performance. You may then make adjustments, such as taking

EXHIBIT 5-8. Multiclass Decision Tree for Each Base Product

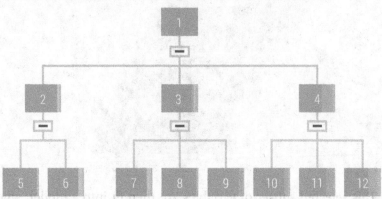

out certain predictors if the business landscape has changed since the historical data was collected or changing model parameters to increase sensitivity.

As an example, for the payments company, we started with the more than 200 variables (from about 200 hypotheses). We divided the training sample into as many subsamples as the base products that the current product merchant uses to take payment. We used variable selection to narrow this down to the top 60 variables and logistic regression to identify the top 35. We then built one multiclass decision tree per segment (see Exhibit 5-8). A multiclass decision tree has more than two discrete values in the dependent variable, like Product A, Product B, Product C, etc., for NBP. In the final set of decision trees, we used 30-odd predictors to produce rules that could be scored in the database. A rule, for example, could look like, "If the merchant used base product A, had annual revenue greater than $500,000, called customer service more than three times in last six months, and has had more than $20,000 in losses in last six months, then NBP = Product Y; expected annual incremental profit (EIP) on adoption = $300."

The model produced many such rules that were then used to score all the current merchants in the database, so that each merchant had an NBP and an EIP. These two values were then used by marketing and product managers for outbound campaigns and by customer service representative for inbound upsell.

Step 5: Recommendations

This last stage of the BADIR framework is where recommendations from the model are presented to the stakeholders for action. This could involve model deployment, such as scoring the model logic in the database, as with NBP scores, or taking the learnings to fix issues, as with a churn model. A churn model is often not scored in the database because the learnings from the model are used to fix churn drivers, for example, bad customer service experience.

Predictive analytics projects tend to be larger in scope and impact than business analytics projects, so you may need to make many "final presentations" customized to different groups of stakeholders. Scoring the model and making many presentations to different audiences are the key differences between predictive and business analytics at this stage.

For the payments company, we presented the final findings to our stakeholder—the head of product and marketing. It consisted of seven main slides, leading with the executive summary, and a thick appendix with all the details of the model. On getting the thumbs-up from our stakeholders, we deployed the NBP model in the database. The marketing team was the first to use the model in a campaign to upsell the most profitable product. As a result of the model, they knew for the first time to whom specifically to upsell that product. They also maintained a control sample, where a random set of the merchants was also sent the offer. The NBP segment had a sixfold conversion as compared to the control sample. In addition, the adopters from the NBP segment delivered 1.5 times the profits on adoption. The model was an instant success and delivered more than $20 million in incremental profits over the course of the year for just the marketing team. The NBP model was eventually also used by other departments, including inbound customer service call.

Predictive Analytics Is Powerful, but Beware of Overuse

As you can see from the use cases above, predictive analytics is one of the tools to keep in your toolkit. It has power, but it must be used ju-

EXHIBIT 5-9. When to Use Predictive Analytics

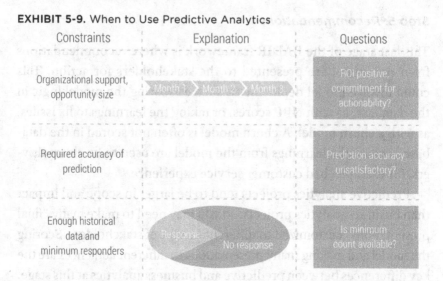

Constraints	Explanation	Questions
Organizational support, opportunity size	Month 1 > Month 2 > Month 3	ROI positive, commitment for actionability?
Required accuracy of prediction		Prediction accuracy unsatisfactory?
Enough historical data and minimum responders	Response / No response	Is minimum count available?

diciously (see Exhibit 5-9). Predictive analytics is resource and time intensive—to the tune of 10 to 20 times that of simple analytics. It requires advanced skills and tools, historical data, operationalization, live validation, and constant maintenance. That is the reason not to use predictive analytics preemptively to solve every business problem. When done right, business analytics lays the foundation for predictive analytics by uncovering opportunities. And, it needs to be a sizable opportunity with the promise of significant returns and with support from the organization before it makes sense to use predictive analytics.

Here is an example where business analytics triumphed over predictive analytics. One of our financial B2B clients asked us to look into its risk policy and its impact on the customer experience. The risk team required that customers verify their identity and provide additional documentation once they reached a specified credit limit. Customers found this requirement frustrating, and it accounted for a $12 million churn annually. To save their customers from this experience, the risk team was building a survival model (a predictive analytics technique) to predict the time it will take for each customer to reach the credit limit, so the company could proactively ask for additional documentation from the customers and dedicate agent time to handle the incoming documents. The model was expected to take three to four months to build, and our project was going to use the predicted time as input in our impact analysis.

Based on our experience working with credit limits, we asked for permission to build something quickly so we could make progress. Using the correlation analysis (a business analytics technique) with the BADIR framework, within 10 days we came up with a simple logic that correctly predicted 80 percent of those who were going to hit the credit limit in the next 3 months. We shared the findings and logic, and we then embarked on the impact project. The risk team quickly adopted and began operationalizing our logic to use as a prediction mechanism. The survival model project was scrapped. It is true that it would have predicted the time to limit with greater accuracy and would have done so at an individual customer level, but our prediction at an aggregated level was sufficient for what the risk team was really trying to do. It saved the risk team four months, as well as associated costs and resources, using the simpler method. Additionally, they could start saving on that $12 million churn and reduce friction for their customers right away.

Marketers, product managers, or operations managers equipped with the BADIR Data-to-Decisions framework and access to data can optimize 80 percent of their day-to-day workflow on their own (as in the example above), without having to rely on scarce and expensive analytics resources. For the remaining 20 percent, where the potential ROI justifies the use of predictive techniques, they can work with their analytics counterparts. This is the picture of a well-functioning organization competing on analytics. In contrast, when organizations and their leaders are misled by the hype around Big Data and predictive analytics, they end up investing lopsidedly on advanced data analytics tools and resources, often resulting in poor ROI.[4]

Additional Resources on Predictive Analytics

Here are some of our recommended readings, activities, and resources on predictive analytics for practitioners.

- Read a book or primer on predictive analytics. We recommend Olivia Parr Rudd's *Data Mining Cookbook: Modeling Data for Marketing, Risk, and Customer Relationship Management* (Wiley, 2000).
- Read the fifth edition of Lora Delwiche and Susan Slaughter, *The Little SAS Book: A Primer* (SAS Institute, 2012) if you are an SAS user.
- Learn to program in R (a free statistical package) with free on-line courses by portals like Coursera.
- Learn with free statistical tools, like KNIME, to start building models visually.
- Take a one- to five-day professional training course on business impact through analytics to effectively engage with data scientists to drive impact for your business.[5] You should not be building models hands-on, unless you are training to become a data scientist. Predictive modeling is fairly complex and has many pitfalls, which sometimes trip up even trained statisticians.

Finally, we do not recommend that anyone learn predictive analytics by attending analytics conferences and reading blogs. Beware that a lot of misinformation is out there, as it is a hot keyword that some vendors are misusing to their advantage. The best way to learn is by building the models with supervised guidance from an experienced modeler.

We have mentioned a few data and analytics tools. In the following chapter, we will look at them more closely and how you can determine what you need.

IN A NUTSHELL

- BADIR can maximize the potential of predictive analytics that otherwise can become a statistical exercise.
- Predictive analytics is a powerful tool that can generate significant business outcome. But it is resource and time intensive. Use it judiciously and only when the ROI can be justified.

SIX

Data and Analytics Tools

THIS CHAPTER WILL TALK ABOUT:

Four categories of business intelligence (BI), and analytics tools.

Factors to consider while deciding on the best tools for your need.

Commonly used tools in each category.

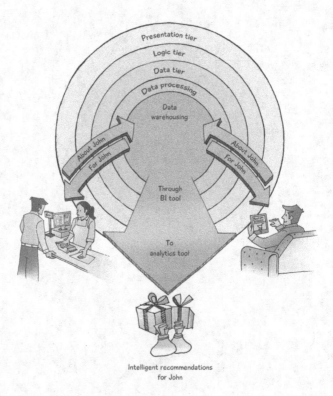

Intelligent recommendations
for John

Fernando has just recently joined StartMatrix, a gaming company, as the Head of Product Development. He asks his team for the product dashboard to quickly understand the dynamics of the business. The team members reluctantly pull a dashboard for him and starts explaining the dynamics of their business, the business model, and more. It is a freemium business model, making most of its money from the whales (the high spenders) and some from advertising. As Fernando digs deeper, he starts to ask pointed questions and maneuvers the report's drag-and-drop mechanism. At this point, things start to crumble. "Do we really have only $2.68 of average spending from the paying base?" "The report shows that most of the base has been acquired through a tablet, whereas the first set of products was not even available outside of a personal computer." The team confesses that it really doesn't trust the data: "To get the average spend, we need to look at a different report coming out of our financial system, but that data doesn't include new users since last month." And so, the conversation developed. By the end of the meeting, Fernando and his team agreed that they simply couldn't trust any of the numbers they had.

I n this company, even the small percentage of accurate data lost its credibility because it was mixed in with so much overwhelmingly inaccurate data. As you can imagine, since the team members didn't trust the data, they couldn't make decisions based on it. To learn about their customers and products, they created new datasets from controlled tests or experiments and analyzed those instead rather than the historical data. The big problem was that without strong hypotheses drawn from historical data, most of those tests were not revealing breakthrough insights that would drive up engagement for their product. In this case, an analytics maturity assessment found that, not surprisingly, their data maturity was very immature. This was simply the biggest obstacle in the way of their using data to better understand their customers' use of their product. They needed a new information architecture, a modified data storage system, and a business intelligence tool.

In business analytics, the most important thing is the right methodology. Even a simple tool like Excel can work well for solving 80 percent of business problems. However, as a business professional, you do need good, clean data that can be accessed easily for the analysis to show results. This chapter explains what tools exist for storing, reporting, and analyzing data to enhance the data maturity of an organization (see Exhibit 6-1). If you know your data is flawed or if you have trouble pulling your own data, the know-how from this chapter will help you understand the issue and have a meaningful conversation with the right person. This will hopefully get you on the path to easy access of clean data. In addition, you gain the perspective of the challenges facing a data scientist, as you work alongside one to achieve your business goals.

There are four broad categories of data and analytics tools:

1. Data storage and processing
2. Business intelligence or reporting
3. Business analytics
4. Advanced analytics

DATA STORAGE AND PROCESSING TOOLS

Data storage and processing has five components: presentation tier, logic tier, data tier, data processing, and data warehouse.

Presentation Tier

As shown in the chapter opening illustration, the presentation tier occurs when a customer interacts with the business and generates data. The data could be of various types—customer data, business transactions, web and mobile activity data, and so on. Here's an example. A customer, John, walks into a bank and provides all the details required to open a checking account. When the bank employee enters his in-

EXHIBIT 6-1. Typical Data Flow in an Organization

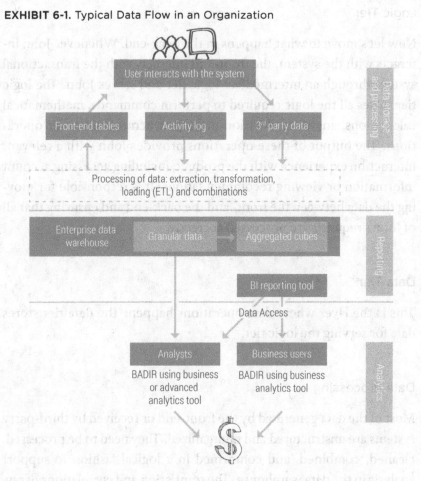

formation into the system, the data is stored in the data tier, which eventually gets written to a data warehouse through a batch ETL process. The transactional system takes in the data and creates a row or perhaps many rows of information about John. It assigns John an identification number. When John walks to the teller and deposits money into his account, the corresponding field in the data tier is updated. Later, when John logs onto his online account to check the balance, this generates web activity, and his row is updated again. If John transfers money to someone, transactional information is checked against his balance, the transfer is executed and then his records are updated again.

Logic Tier

Now let's move to what happens in the back-end. Whenever John interacts with the system, the front-end interacts with the transactional system through an intermediate logic tier and serves John. The logic tier stores all the logic required to perform commands, mathematical calculations, analytical decision-making structure, and other operations. The output of these operations provides John with a relevant interaction experience with the product, including accessing account information or viewing recommendations. It is responsible for moving the data between the front- and the back-end and ensuring that all of John's requests are processed correctly.

Data Tier

This is the layer where data operations happen. The data tier stores data for serving the logic tier.

Data Processing

Most of the data generated by the front-end or received by third-party systems are unstructured and unorganized. They need to be processed, cleaned, combined, and conformed in a logical fashion to support analysis in the data warehouse. The translation and correlations of raw data into base metric and business entities (how much, by when, where, who, etc.) is a key initial step in the application of business rules and logic to support measuring and reporting in a structured fashion. These operations called ETL (extraction, transformation, and loading) are done in regular intervals to keep the database updated with all of John's activity.

Data Warehouse

After ETL is done, the structured data flows into various tables in the enterprise data warehouse (EDW). EDW stores all information from any number of systems in one place, does not interfere with transactional data, and enables a single version of truth as opposed to having numerous independent files and tables. EDW also enables availability of historical data. EDW might have specific tables for specific types of information. Examples of such tables include a customer table with demographics, a snapshot of activity, a risk and marketing profile, or a transaction table with information such as transaction amount, number of transactions, and type of product purchased.

A data collection and storage system should have the capacity to handle a large quantity of data, process it efficiently, and allow analysts to quickly access it. Many organizations use relational data storage technologies, such as IBM DB2, Microsoft SQL Server, Oracle, and Teradata, to support these structured and traditional datasets. As the demand for data and data storage has risen, new players have introduced technologies promising lower cost solutions that scale easily and have low latency response times. One of the manifestations of this phenomenon is Big Data. Big Data came on the data warehouse and business intelligence radar 10 years ago as a catchall for any methodology and technology involved in handling large and complex datasets. For the purpose of this discussion, we will narrow the scope of Big Data to technologies that allow the storage, processing, and querying of terabytes to petabytes of data. Traditional databases, such as Netezza and Teradata, already solved this through their distributed processing paradigm. However, while scaling using these technologies is achievable, it requires massive proprietary hardware and licensing costs. New computing platforms, such as Hadoop, which is open source, scales through inexpensive commodity hardware, and supports both structured (tables) and unstructured data, is the new driving force behind Big Data. Companies such as Yahoo and Facebook pioneered and contributed to the evolution of Hadoop to support the petabyte scale datasets they required to power their sites. This technology is now being used beyond these digital companies as an alternative to traditional data processing.

From the analytics perspective, the most critical aspect of data storage and processing is its overall information architecture. Information

architecture is the design of how information should flow, what gets
stored, and where. In Fernando and StarMatrix's case, information
re-architecture was the first action we advocated even before the right
data storage and processing system was set in place.

BUSINESS INTELLIGENCE OR REPORTING TOOLS

BI or reporting tools enable quick and easy visual access to aggregated
data in the form of static and dynamic reports. Its aggregated and visual output enables business users and executives to self-serve on data
without the need for an expert.

Often, businesses mistakenly overload these tools by connecting
them to granular, nonaggregated data, making the BI tool sluggish
in its performance. This makes the tool unusable, and business users
again find the need to approach a data analyst to get the relevant data
based on what they are looking to monitor and manage. Raw granular
data needs to be aggregated in order to maintain fast access to data
through the BI tools. Aggregation is a two-part process.

1. **Create relevant subsets of data:** Analyze only the last three
   years of data. This analysis would be by week and month rather
   than by day to reduce size.
2. **Roll up to appropriate granularity:** Granular data can have
   thousands of metrics. For the user to easily access appropriate
   information, this needs to be culled down to a manageable
   number (100-300) by prioritization and aggregation. This is a
   function of the business question the user is trying to answer
   and for which the metrics need to be prioritized. The first thing
   is to identify the top 10 to 15 strategic projects for a department
   or company using the 3 Key Questions framework (discussed
   in Chapter 8). The next is to use BADIR to answer the business
   questions behind these strategic projects and then lay out the
   hypotheses to get to the top 100 to 300 metrics that matter the
   most to the business.

This rolled-up subset of metrics is what is stored as aggregated cubes to which the BI tool can connect, access, and visualize far more efficiently than the granular data. Once the back-end BI cube is set up appropriately, all business professionals who have been well trained on these tools can build their own report.

A plethora of tools are available in the market for reporting. To make an informed choice, use the following guidelines to acquire the tool that satisfies most of your needs. IBM, Oracle, Teradata, Microsoft, and SAP have their application-specific tool. Some of the other commonly used tools in the market are Tableau, Datameer, MicroStrategy, and Qliktech. Cloud and open-source BI vendors, such as Birst, Good-Data, and Jaspersoft, have gained traction in recent years as less expensive and more customizable alternatives to enterprise BI technologies. In choosing the right tool for reporting, the following are key.

Visualization

Data visualization has evolved from mere bar charts and pie charts to a science of its own, with multitudes of devoted bloggers. The right visualizations can quickly and intuitively highlight insights and anomalies in your data. This is a powerful tool for analysts in data discovery work or for creating executive briefings. In evaluating visualization capabilities, assess if the tool has, out of the box, a rich and flexible graphing and visualization library. Does it have any recommendation functionalities to propose the right graph for the right data set?

Channel

Accessibility and shareability of data is key in our mobile, local, and social-driven society. Are reports accessible from a comprehensive set of channels and platforms like mobile, cloud, PC, mail, text, alerts, tweets, and other social media activity?

Speed and Ease

The success of the business intelligence tool is in large part measured by adoption. Are reports quick to generate and easy to access? Is it easy to navigate? Is it easy to share reports in required formats? Does it have an intuitive graphical user interface (GUI) for the user to be able to manipulate the report easily, for example using a drag-and-drop functionality?

Integration with Other Tools

While data integration and combination is usually the domain of data processing, the ability to access different data sets quickly means faster time to value for your data, even if it is a one-off solution. Does this tool have the ability to seamlessly connect and consolidate data from relational and Big Data tools? Does it have the ability to combine data from multiple tools, such as sales transactions, from a relational database with customer data from Salesforce.com?

Data and User Limitations

Expect your user base and data size to grow, and do some estimates and planning on the user scale and data scale you will have in three-to-five years. The scalability of your BI solution should match your expectations. Does this tool pose any limitations on datasets and number of users? Does its performance decrease with increase in size or complexity of the data?

Cost

What costs are associated with the tool, such as licensing, implementation, and operation?

Ease of Deployment and Maintenance

Deployment and maintenance costs can add up quickly and outpace the upfront software cost in a matter of months. How easy, quick, and affordable is the tool to implement? What type of support is available from the vendor and from internal resources? Requesting a total cost of ownership from the BI vendor as part of your evaluation may provide additional color here.

Analysis Capability

Most business intelligence solutions have some level of analysis capabilities, which can help simplify the workflow of analysts who can access and analyze data using the same interface. Does this tool have the capability to do simple analytics, such as aggregate, correlation, and trend analyses? Does it provide simple statistical functions, such as averages and standard deviation?

Information Design Capability

Does it have data modeling capability, such as design of star schema, dimensions, KPIs, and so on?

BUSINESS ANALYTICS TOOLS

These tools enable users to apply the simpler business analytics methodologies visually to the data on hand. These methodologies, including aggregate analysis, correlation analysis, and trend analysis, were discussed in Chapters 3 and 4. Any business professional who has access to data should be able to analyze it on their own using a good business analytics tool. They can find hidden patterns, explain fluctuations, size opportunities, and make high-level projections.

Our tool of choice for simple analytics is, drumroll, Microsoft Excel. It is the spreadsheet application in the Microsoft Office package. It is by far the most widely used tool for business analytics and has seen some powerful improvements and plug-ins in recent years that have enabled more sophisticated analysis. Excel is ideal for business users, who do not handle large datasets or perform complex analytics.

Excel uses a traditional table structure, that is, rows and columns of data. It can easily export to a variety of tools. It can be connected to database tables, such as Microsoft Access tables, and has plug-ins that can connect it to relational and nonrelational databases. It is typically used for aggregate analysis, correlation and trend analysis, sizing and estimation, and simple predictive modeling and time series forecasting. Recent versions have seen the addition of advanced statistical and math functionalities as well. It is fairly easy to visually represent the analysis in Excel, which has static and dynamic graphing options. It is multiplatform and can be accessed and operated on PC, in the cloud, and on mobile devices.

If you are a business user with access to data through a reporting tool that does not enable analytics, we recommend exporting your dataset using CSV file format into Excel, which can then be used as your analysis tool.

Excel is really easy to pick up. Its popularity stems from a very intuitive and easy-to-learn graphical user interface. It has an easy learning curve of one to two weeks, so it can be put to use quickly for less sophisticated business analysis and reporting. The one limitation is that it can handle only a maximum of one million rows. However, recent extensions, like Power Pivot, extend that to 10 million rows.

In addition to Excel, many of the BI tools mentioned above, including Tableau, Datameer, and MicroStrategy, have decent business analytics capability. Many advanced analytics tools we talk about below also have a starter product geared toward quick visualization and business analytics.

ADVANCED ANALYTICS TOOLS

Further up the ladder sit the advanced analytics tools. Over time, many tools were developed and used in schools and universities and then adopted by statisticians and analysts in the corporate world. A few have matured with the market and become mainstream; a few still find application in niche industries, academia, government, research institutions, and trading floors; others were acquired as part of vertical integration by larger players, such as IBM, SAP, and Teradata, and have grown into billion dollar entities.

Key considerations in choosing the right tool for advanced analytics are visualization capability, type of data it can handle, cost, integration with other tools, data and user limitation, and operational efficiency. In addition, the following two attributes should be considered.

1. **Ease of Learning:** Does it have a graphical user interface? How much coding is required to perform analyses? What are the cost and availability of training and trained resources?
2. **Type of Analytics:** In addition to simple analysis, does it have advanced analytics capabilities to do predictive analytics, time series forecasting, segmentation (clustering), life-cycle analysis, and scenario modeling? Does it have the capability to do simulations like Monte Carlo?

There are many advanced analytics tools on the market, including KNIME, R, SAS Enterprise Miner, and Angoss Knowledge Studio. Of these, KNIME and R are free. KNIME is a GUI tool, while R is not.

KNIME

For the analytics professional, who is well versed with advanced statistical concepts, KNIME is a user-friendly graphical software which is available at no cost. Although it is not as stable as other software, it is still quite functional and is useful for small teams with no budget for these advanced tools.

R

R is also coming up as a tool for choice for many data miners, but it does have a steep learning curve as it is not graphical.

SAS

The SAS Enterprise Miner is world-class software used by many Fortune 100 companies. It is graphical, but its steep pricing makes it a valid option only for medium and large enterprises. SAS has a cheaper, lightweight option in JMP software, which is also visual, but has some data size limitations.

Angoss

Angoss-Knowledge studio is a GUI-based tool that makes decision trees a breeze. Because it is visual, the results are easy to understand. This also is a good option for Enterprise, as it is expensive.

Not every advanced analytics tool has everything. Costs and the extent of the learning curve can vary significantly. So, make your decision based on your particular needs and situation. These tools are used almost exclusively by expert data analysts and scientists because of the depth of knowledge required to work with them effectively. Business users would ideally be working with their analytics counterpart to resolve the 20 percent of problems that require advanced analytics.

IN A NUTSHELL

- If, as a business professional, you don't have easy access to data through a visual BI tool, work with your head of analytics to quickly enable that.
- If the data at your disposal is not accurate, it is an urgent call to look at the information architecture and data tools.
- Once you have access to data, Microsoft Excel is your best friend to quickly get insights from data that will help solve 80 percent of business problems.

3

LEADERSHIP TOOLKIT

Analytics and Leadership

THIS CHAPTER WILL TALK ABOUT:

The role of leadership to build a data-enabled organization and team.

Four key attributes by which a leader can assess an organization's analytics maturity.

Capital One Financial Corp.   (NYSE:COF)   Add to portfolio

66.67 -0.01 (-0.02%)

After Hours: 66.41 -0.26 (-0.39%)
Aug 23, 4:55PM EDT
NYSE real-time data - Disclaimer
Currency in USD

Range	66.10 - 67.06	Div/yield	0.30/1.80
52 week	50.21 - 70.00	EPS	7.44
Open	67.06	Shares	585.34M
Vol / Avg.	1.15M/2.66M	Beta	1.70
Mkt cap	39.02B	Inst. own	90%
P/E	8.97		

Compare: Enter ticker here   Add   ☑ Dow Jones ☑ S&P 500 ☐ DFS ☐ AXP ☐ CASH ☐ NBCB ☐ FPLPY ☐ BKU « less
☐ FIS ☑ NYSE:C ☑ NYSE:BAC ☑ NYSE.WFC ☑ NYSE.JPM

Zoom: 1d 5d 1m 3m 6m YTD 1y 5y 10y All
Nov 25, 1994 - Aug 23, 2013

1995 1996 1997 1998 1999 2000 2001 2002 2003 2004 2005 2006 2007 2008 2009 2010 2011 2012 201

Settings | Technicals | ⊷ Link to this view   Volume delayed by 15 mins
1.NYSE:JPM +581.29% 2.NYSE:WFC +627.83% 3.Dow Jones +284.23% 4.NYSE:BAC +16.33% 5.NYSE:C -3.41% 6. S&P 500 +259.85% 7. COF +1143.40

Richard Fairbank, the current CEO of Capital One[1] is rumored to have remarked that on a good day, he expects 7 out of 10 decisions to actually perform as per plan. In the 1980s, all financial services companies were issuing one-size-fits-all credit cards. They charged all their customers the same 19.4 percent APR and a $20 annual fee. At that time, Fairbank and Nigel Morris, the cofounders of Capital One, had the idea to leverage customer data to create customer segments and give different credit card offers to different segments. Thus, they conquered the subprime market by making credit cards available to a huge new customer base for the first time, thereby revolutionizing the lending industry.

This data-enabled innovation had a profound impact on the company. From 1996 to 2004, Capital One's annual return on equity and earnings-per-share growth were both more than 20 percent. In 2008, when the economy crashed, so did Capital One, but its recovery was a different story. While stock performance of other diversified banks, like Citibank, Bank of America, JPMorgan Chase, and Wells Fargo struggled to return to their former glory, Capital One outperformed all of them. It also outperformed the Dow Jones and S&P 500.

Richard Fairbank is a data-driven leader. A data-driven leader:

- Is committed to learning about his or her customer and all dynamics that affect the customer to drive growth and innovation.
- Inherently believes that data will help drive superior business decisions and outcomes.

In that capacity, as both the catalysts and the engines of a company, data-enabled leaders choose to be evidence-based decision makers. Use the toolkit in this section to power your leadership with analytics. To begin, you need to assess and build your organization's analytics maturity.

DEFINING YOUR ORGANIZATION'S ANALYTICS MATURITY

Your organization needs to be strong in four areas for you to successfully leverage analytics: leadership, analytics talent, decision making, and data maturity. If your organization has accumulated tons of data, but the product and marketing teams cannot leverage it to achieve perceivable growth, that is a sign that one of the four areas is problematic. Look at your organization in terms of these areas and strive to correct any shortcomings.

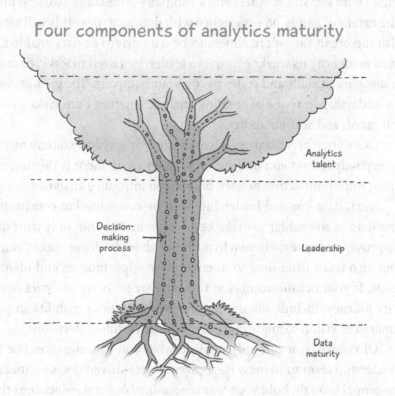

Four components of analytics maturity

Component 1: Leadership

> *From the beginning, Richard Fairbank and his team set up Capital One with data and analytics as its backbone, and they built the company culture and talent around it.*

McKinsey's 2011 report on Big Data states that "analyzing large data sets . . . will become a key basis of competition, underpinning new waves of productivity growth, innovation, and consumer surplus. . . . Leaders in every sector will have to grapple with the implications of Big Data—not just a few data-oriented managers."[2] Data analytics is not just a passing fad; the McKinsey researchers anticipate an "exponential growth in data for the foreseeable future."

To enable your company to analyze all this data, the first step should be a detailed assessment of your organization, involving interviews with key stakeholders and a company-wide survey to determine the extent of hands-on experience with data analytics. This will establish the organization's readiness to be data driven or data enabled, as well as identify its weaknesses. As a leader, you need to leverage many management skills and styles to run your company. The greatest gaps in leadership in terms of creating analytics maturity are vision, commitment, and accountability.

Does your organization have a vision or a vision statement that everybody knows and understands? Such a statement is the first and most important action needed before you introduce analytics.

Next, data-enabled leadership must be committed to consistently use data as an enabler to make key decisions. They not only trust data to prove/disprove their own hypotheses about business opportunities but also learn from data to uncover new opportunities and identify gaps. If your organization is in the early stages of its analytics maturity journey, include the development of analytics capability in your multiyear vision to guide company-wide investment decisions.

Of course, you can only manage what you can measure. For the leadership team to harness the power of data-driven decision making to propel growth, hold your teams accountable for the decisions they make. Whether you use zero-sum budgeting, balanced scorecards, or other ways to track a leadership team's decisions and performance, there needs to be a quantifiable accountability within all ranks of the organization.

There may be other ways to optimize decisions—luck, gut, religion, magic—but none of these deliver consistent, repeatable results. Basing decisions on measureable data and documented analysis can help you make smarter decisions that lead to consistent, repeatable success you can build on, learn from, and use to grow. It has 7 out of 10 times for Richard Fairbank!

Component 2: Analytics Talent

Capital One has a unique way of acquiring analytics talent at the junior and middle management levels, engaging people with strong analytical skills for most job functions that are involved in making high-impact decisions. The process includes a written quantitative screening test, two rounds of case interviews, and two rounds of behavioral interviews. The quantitative test is so difficult that even some candidates with high GMAT scores could not pass. For the case interviews, each interviewer receives some formal training so the results will be comparable. In the debriefing meeting, all interviewers share their scores and discuss in detail if the scores have a wide variance. Finally, they correlate employee performance on the job, that is, their annual performance ratings, with the scores received in interviewing process. They have found that highest scoring candidates do, in fact, perform better on the job than others.

Leadership sets the goals, but it does not directly deliver outcome. That requires analytics talent, and not just in your analysts. The best first step is to bring in a senior analytics leader, affording that person influence and a say in the organization's functions and strategy.

The McKinsey Big Data report also projects that by 2018 there will be a shortage of 140,000 to 190,000 data analysts and up to 1.5 million analytical business managers to work on the trove of data that businesses will be gathering. In fact, a clear talent gap already exists. This is both the challenge and the opportunity.[3] This gap can be closed as more business professionals garner Data-to-Decisions skills and as analytical skills become a core personnel need. Many specialized analytics agencies are filling this through training and recruitment services.

In 2011, an Accenture study found that U.S. workers, under pressure to improve skills, were quick to add technology skills but slow in adding problem solving, analytical, or managerial skills.[4] Thus, employers should invest in empowering business professionals with much needed data-to-decision skills, which will cover two of the three skill gaps, that is, problem solving and analytical skills.

Analytics Talent on the Business Side

Whether you are a business professional making decisions as part of your daily workflow or a business owner or leader, you need to use data to find insights that can drive better results for you and your organization. Whether planning for seasonal inventory for a boutique or staffing a retail outlet, understanding data trends, such as past sales or daily flow of foot traffic, will help optimize inventory and resources.

Business professionals involved in decision making need easy access to data through some kind of tool like Tableau, Business Object, or MicroStrategy. They are also need to develop three key skills:

- **Hands-On Business Analytics and Testing**: Business professionals need an understanding of and hands-on experience with a data-to-decisions framework that combines data science and decision science. For data science, they should know basic business analytics methodologies, be able to perform operations in Excel, and have a basic understanding of A/B testing. This would help solve 80 percent of their business problems.

- **Working Effectively with Analysts**: They need to work effectively with data scientists and analysts to support their hands-on effort (on the 80 percent of solvable problems) and work in partnership with them for more complex problems requiring advanced analytics.
- **Introductory Advanced Analytics**: They need an overall understanding of predictive analytics, including regression, decision tree, and segmentation analytics, to effectively engage with the analyst as the need arises.

Analytics Talent on the Data Side

The analytics professional also needs data and decision science skills to analyze data, as well as develop the interpersonal and business skills needed to bridge the gap from data to business. Most organizations find it challenging to hire people trained in business analytics, as formal analytics education wasn't available until recently. You can, however, cultivate people in-house who show an aptitude for analytics. By investing in analytics training and hiring senior analytics professionals to lead or augment the team, you can move the organization toward analytics maturity.

Data scientists and analyst teams need a combination of these four skills.

- **Hands-On Business Analytics and Testing**: Analysts also need hands-on experience with a data-to-decisions framework that includes basic business analytics methodologies. They especially need strong decision science skills in building alignment using influence and communication for their work to significantly impact the business. If the organization is involved in testing, they need a solid foundation in Test and Learn, also called A/B testing.

- **SQL Skills:** Data analysts must be skilled at pulling and collating data from multiple sources. Experience in writing SQL queries and exposure to tools like Teradata and Oracle are important. Some understanding of Big Data tools, such as Hadoop, is also helpful.
- **Hands-On Advanced Analytics:** Analysts require hands-on facility with advanced techniques, such as predictive analytics, which includes regression and decision tree, time series, clustering and, optionally as the business requires, text analytics.
- **Stat Tools:** To perform advanced statistical analysis, they need experience with one or more statistical tools, such as SAS, R, SPSS, or Knime.

Analytics team members have varying combinations of the above skills. For example, a data analyst is strong in the second skill, but has an understanding of the first. A business analytics professional would be strong in the first, with understanding of the second and third. A predictive analytics professional is strong in the third and fourth, with a good command of the first. Few professionals are strong in all four areas, so often you will need to staff the team with people who have a mix of these skills.

Component 3: Decision Making

Capital One also has a remarkable decision-making process, which is necessary to a data-driven organization. The company has a rigorous planning process for evaluating each new idea. The product or marketing manager presenting the idea has to analyze past customer data in estimating the performance of the proposed project and also map scenarios and the risks involved in each to safeguard the company against financial loss. Once an idea is approved, it is piloted or tested before a full roll out occurs. In addition to a forward-looking planning process, Capital One also has a system-

atic review process. After a project is launched and results start streaming in, leaders have to monitor the launch to assess whether it is going as expected. If not, they will need to change in flight or kill the project. All these decisions are reviewed not only with the respective senior management, but also in a formal review process across different groups.

There are many opportunities within business functions, such as strategy, marketing, product, operations, design, and innovation, to use data analysis to make better decisions. A company's marketing budget allocation, for example, provides a good opportunity to do this, as there are so many ways to divide the budget and so many target groups and subgroups to address. Are you trying to grow lifetime value of a customer or bring new customers on board? Most companies see the many possibilities, but do not have nearly enough budget to address them. This is where data-driven decision making pays off.

For instance, CEOs are not placed to make individual decisions across all functions and levels of the organization. An effective decision-making structure within a company will empower business heads, as well as the rank and file, to make these decisions through closeness to their business context and clarity of the company's vision.

The solution is to set up a transparent decision-making process that everybody in the organization understands. At a strategic level, such a process makes clear the:

- Kinds of projects that get funded.
- Evaluation criteria for choosing one project over another. This can include financial and nonfinancial measures, such as customer satisfaction, innovation, sustainability, and community impact.

The decision-making process requires:

1. A process for collecting all the proposed initiatives, along with information about their expected investment and returns. This can take the form of a strategic planning input document in

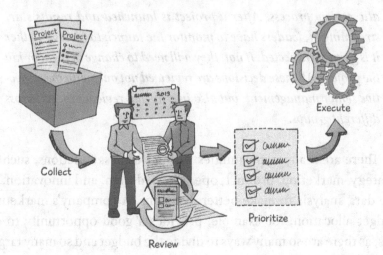

which key contributors get to pitch their ideas. The initiatives are then vetted from this pool. Companies like PayPal do it annually; smaller companies may do it monthly or quarterly. But all projects submitted by the required date are considered.

2. A team of stakeholders to review new initiatives at a regular interval, such as a monthly or quarterly formal planning-and-review process. At a review meeting, stakeholders go over results from the last set of decisions, evaluating and learning from them to make decisions about new initiatives. Typically, review and planning happens in the same cycle. Although a monthly or quarterly cycle is recommended, some start-ups do this on a daily basis. Whatever cycle you choose, make sure there is enough time to incorporate learnings from the last set of decisions in the next planning cycle.

3. A set of criteria to prioritize one project over another. The 3 Key Questions framework (discussed in Chapter 8) is a helpful tool for identifying the Key Performance Indicators (KPIs) and their drivers. Answers to these questions come in handy when identifying the top projects the organization should invest in and the criteria for deciding.

4. A clear description how projects will be executed, including process, criteria, and metrics. Every decision maker in the organization should be exposed to the plan for implementing new projects, the criteria behind the decision to proceed, the metric each project is expected to drive, and how that metric relates to the organization's overriding priorities and KPIs.

Component 4: Data Maturity

Another thing that stands out about Capital One is its investment in establishing a solid foundation of data maturity. It is one of few organizations in which most of the data is clean by the time it reaches the data warehouse. In fact, data is so clean and reliable that when there is a break in a trend, Capital One does not need to validate the data again. Rather, such a break means something has surely happened. Early in the 2000s, Capital One upgraded its systems to simplify and integrate its hundreds of independent systems, as well as its enterprise data warehouse, into one unified warehouse. Company leaders picked the top 500 employees from all job functions to be part of that project for 18 months, ensuring that the top performers and most knowledgeable people were working on this key strategic initiative.

Our many examples prove that investment in data analytics pays off. To reap that payback, though, a data team must be able to collect and store the appropriate data and ensure seamless access by analysts and business users alike. The organization can then generate the kind of insights that result in winning decisions and successful strategies. This is the source of the analytics payback, the ROI we refer to so much.

Analytics starts with a solid foundation of good data. By good data, we mean accurate data, collected in a timely way, securely stored in a way that both protects the integrity of the data and ensures ready and easy access to it. Organizations that have invested in infrastructure with appropriate data collection and storage processes have laid the groundwork to start leveraging data as an asset. Bad data—incomplete, riddled with errors, inconsistent, and contradictory—can severely impair an organization's ability to learn about its customers and products through data. It can also severely affect the trust that decision makers need to have on what the data is showing them.

Data maturity consists of four primary components: infrastructure, access, usability, and the instrumentation process.

Data maturity relies foremost on a nimble data infrastructure that scales appropriately and supports the kinds of access the organization needs. Additionally, as analytics is performed and there is a need for previously unavailable data or metrics, an agile infrastructure can quickly enable capturing of new data fields and sources. This process is called instrumentation. The new data source or field can then feed into an existing and well-grounded data infrastructure.

Data maturity

- ☑ Infrastructure
- ☑ Access
- ☑ Usability
- ☑ Instrumentation process

Analysts and business professionals are users with distinct and different data access needs. Consequently, they rely on the usability of the infrastructure. Business professionals should have easy access to limited, aggregated data through a business intelligence (BI) tool, such as Tableau or Business Object. Data analysts require direct access to an enterprise data warehouse (EDW), where detailed underlying user and event level data is stored. This access is likely through SQL querying or a comparable protocol. The data infrastructure needs to support both of these kinds of data access.

The qualities of an effective data infrastructure are as below.

- Its design and architecture are open and flexible yet secure.
- It can scale to handle more data and users.
- It can expand to handle more and different types of data.
- It delivers the performance needed to handle complex queries and large volumes of data.

- It can interact with a large and changing number of systems, technologies, and tools.
- It is easily and securely accessible for authorized users, whether data analyst or business user.

Surprisingly, the most difficult aspect of developing an effective data infrastructure is not the choice of hardware or technology, but rather the design and architecture of your information system. If information architecture talent is not available in your organization, hire external consultants to design an information flow that your internal team can understand. Note, however, that there is also no need to overinvest in collecting all the data possible. If you answer the 3 Key Questions appropriately, you and your leadership team will identify the gaps in understanding of your business and highlight the kind of data you do need. And, remember, as your business evolves, so will the data needed. So setting up an instrumentation process is an integral part of data maturity.

Capital One is a poster child for how to set up an analytics-driven organization. The good news is that your organization can be one too. There is a method to this madness, and it can be achieved within your time and budget constraints. The most important thing is to want it, plan for it, and drive toward it. The next chapter discusses how you can lead your organization to compete on analytics.

IN A NUTSHELL

- To best leverage analytics, first assess your organization's analytics maturity.
- The four components of analytics maturity are leadership, analytics talent, decision making, and data maturity.

EIGHT

Competing on Analytics

THIS CHAPTER WILL TALK ABOUT:

3 Key Questions to lay the analytics agenda
for an organization.

Optimal organizational structure for a data-enabled company.

A philosophy professor stood before his class. As the session started, he wordlessly picked up a very large and empty jar and proceeded to fill it with big rocks. He then asked the students if the jar was full. They agreed that it was. He then picked up a box of pebbles and poured them into the jar. He shook the jar lightly. The pebbles, of course, rolled into the open areas between the rocks. He then asked the students again if the jar was full. They agreed it was. The professor next picked up a box of sand and poured it into the jar, which filled up all the remaining spaces. The students unanimously agree that the jar was now full. He then proceeded to fill the jar with beer.

Although well known, this story is worth repeating. The professor likens his analogy to life—the big rocks are the big things in your life, such as family and health. If all else was lost, these things would still fill your life. So, you take care of the big rocks first. We extrapolate this analogy to an organization. The big rocks are the three to five mandates that drive an organization, such as maintaining specific percentages of customer satisfaction, returns on assets, employee retention, and driving stakeholder value. The big rocks shouldn't change often, as they inform a company's goals. The pebbles are the key initiatives that deliver the big rocks; these may change from year to year. The sand is everything else the organization does to achieve and maintain the big rocks. It is important that initiatives and actions within the organization don't compromise these big rocks. And the beer? Well, there's always room for celebration.

A well-formulated analytics agenda helps align the big rocks with the KPIs by managing and recalibrating the drivers of the business. Let us talk about how to create an optimal analytics agenda using the 3 Key Questions framework and then lay out your organizational structure to support this agenda.

PART I: 3 KEY QUESTIONS FRAMEWORK

After conducting an analytics maturity assessment, you have determined that your organization is ready to become data powered. Now the big questions are, "Where do you begin?" and "What do you do with that data?" Clearly, you need an analytics agenda. This chapter guides you through what you can expect to accomplish from your analytics initiatives. Think of it as a high-level analytics plan for the entire business. Most importantly, the 3 Key Questions need to be part of a cross-functional initiative, originating from leadership if it is to be effective (see Exhibit 8-1).

Start by asking the 3 Key Questions of your data and run your business with the resulting insights:

1. How am I doing?
2. What drives my business?
3. Who are my customers, and what are their needs?

EXHIBIT 8-1. The 3 Key Questions Approach

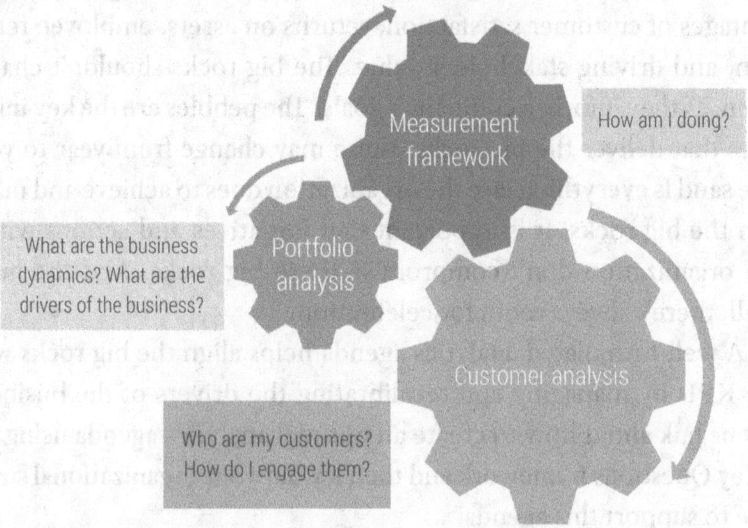

Then, engage across and through your organization to fully understand and build the three pillars of understanding, which are:

1. A measurement framework to answer, "How am I doing?"
2. A portfolio analysis to answer, "What drives my business?"
3. A customer analysis to answer, "Who are my customers, and what are their needs?"

Let's look at each.

First Pillar: Measurement Framework

How am I doing?

The usual response is a financial one—revenue, transaction margins, ROI, and more. There are, however, other ways to answer the question. You could, for example, respond with a balanced scorecard that combines financial information with nonfinancial metrics, such as customer satisfaction and shareholder value.[1] In either case, you are looking to define your primary key metrics, or KPIs, and then identify the secondary and tertiary drivers. These could be individual metrics of business units that are aligned to the overall business goals and priorities.

The measurement framework establishes comprehensive and repeatable steps for evaluating your company's performance in relation to your own stated goals. Once you've created the measurement framework, you can choose the right projects (analytics or otherwise) that are most likely to move your company's KPIs.

The key is to decompose the metrics to a level that can be influenced by projects. As in the example in Exhibit 8-2, the transaction margin can be the KPI. All other metrics, such as revenue, number of churned merchants, etc., are drivers. Here, we derived from the data that reducing the number of churned merchants by x% can increase revenue by y$ and margin by z%. Once this is determined, you can align internal projects, such as churn analysis, to work on those drivers.

EXHIBIT 8-2. Measurement Framework

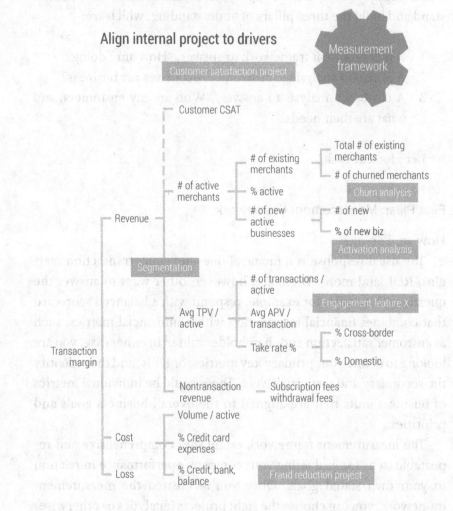

Align internal project to drivers

Measurement frameworks also follow the principles of laying hypotheses for drivers and using analysis to confirm the right drivers within the framework and eliminate those that don't contribute to the KPI. Some levers that are identified are not easy to influence. In Exhibit 8-2, levers such as "average transaction value" cannot be easily changed by an organization. This is an example of a nonpullable lever. You must also identify pullable and nonpullable levers through stakeholder meetings so you can align projects to the pullable levers. In the example, your business should focus on a pullable lever, such as the number of churned merchants, instead of a nonpullable lever, such as average payment value (APV), which is the value of the goods or services purchased.

Second Pillar: Portfolio Analysis

What drives my business?

With this question, you're seeking to understand the dynamics of your business. How do your different products perform relative to each other? What new opportunities can you identify based on relative performance?

Now that you have confirmed the correct drivers from the measurement framework, you can begin to understand the dynamics of your portfolio by observing how these drivers perform when segmented by products or offerings. Generally, you start by reviewing the overall profit and loss (P&L) statement to understand the relative performance of your products, offerings, business unit, or any other segment of your business. Then compare these by creating a series of 2×2 or $2 \times 2 \times 2$ matrices to map your company's portfolio across different metrics.[2]

In the example, the products have been mapped by growth, profit, and relative size. When you have a solid understanding of how your products interact with the marketplace and combine this information with multiple business metrics, such as growth, profitability, size, revenue, penetration, share of wallet, competitive benefit, and customer value, you can determine where your greatest growth potential lies and where the greatest danger of failure lurks (see Exhibit 8-3).

Once you have an informed understanding of your portfolio, you can leverage data to glean insights against your risks and opportunities and boost the projects that will help strengthen your company. For example, by looking at products across growth and profit dynamics in the above figure, you may find a product (Product C) that has high

EXHIBIT 8-3. Portfolio Analysis: Determine the Focus

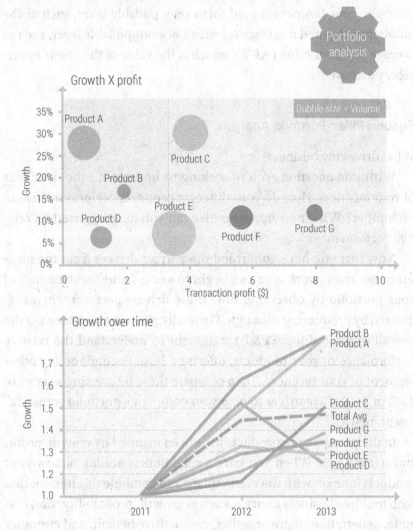

growth and high profits. After thus identifying your golden product or Star, you can build a cross-sell predictive model to identify top customers who are likely to buy the golden product. This is an example of how analysis insight can lead to projects to drive business impact. The matrix can offer further insights, as with Product G, which by definition is a highly profitable cash cow with low growth. Understanding why the growth is below average will help you improve on a product with great potential.

Exhibit 8-4 shows how you can identify projects to work on, based on insights from portfolio analysis.

EXHIBIT 8-4. Portfolio Analysis: Align Internal Projects to the Portfolio

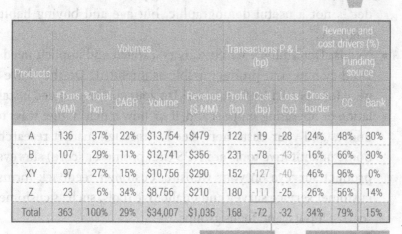

Products	Volumes				Transactions P & L (bp)					Revenue and cost drivers (%) Funding source	
	#Txns (MM)	%Total Txn	CAGR	Volume	Revenue ($ MM)	Profit (bp)	Cost (bp)	Loss (bp)	Cross border	CC	Bank
A	136	37%	22%	$13,754	$479	122	-19	-28	24%	48%	30%
B	107	29%	11%	$12,741	$356	231	-78	-43	16%	66%	30%
XY	97	27%	15%	$10,756	$290	152	-127	-40	46%	96%	0%
Z	23	6%	34%	$8,756	$210	180	-111	-25	26%	56%	14%
Total	363	100%	29%	$34,007	$1,035	168	-72	-32	34%	79%	15%

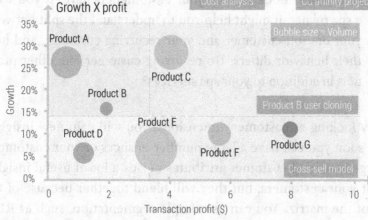

Third Pillar: Customer Analysis

Who are my customers, and what are their needs?

How do they behave? How do they use my products? What do they need? These are the crucial questions in your customer analysis. Customer attributes span several categories, including the following:

- **Demographics:** What are your customer demographics? How many are female? What's the average age? What percentage is married with children? The relevant demographic metrics will depend on your specific products and services. For instance, at Curves, a weight loss center catering primarily to women, gender is not a useful demographic, but age and buying habits might be.
- **Needs:** Determine your customers' explicit and implicit needs. Do they find your product usable as intended? Do they have a need for a particular feature set? Do your customers need installation or operating support and, if so, how much? Other ways to understand your customers' need is through market research. Some quantitative tools are NPS (net promoter score) surveys, product surveys on your website, customer feedback forms, customer service survey and qualitative tools, such as customer service inputs, and focus groups.
- **Behaviors:** Look at how your customers behave. If you were a spa owner, it might help you to understand the split between your one-off customer and your recurring customer, and how their behavior differs. Do recurring customer like other products in addition to your spa services?

By looking at customer dimensions, you will gain new insights. Very soon you can have a large number of slices of your customers. A large matrix of customer attributes means a lot of useful insights about your customers, but they will blend together because of the size of the matrix. You can use simple segmentation, such as RFM (recency, frequency, monetary), or advanced segmentation, such as

EXHIBIT 8-5. Customer Analysis: Identifying Your Customer's Needs

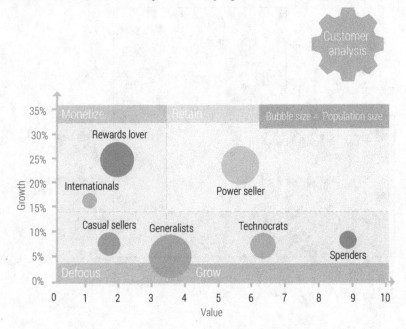

clustering, to segment your customer base into five to seven most meaningful segments. This is how we arrived at the seven segments in the example shown in Exhibit 8-5.

Once you have your customers in meaningful segments, you can plot your customer segment into meaningful 2 × 2s to guide your customer engagement strategy. Exhibit 8-6 shows how to identify projects to engage your customers, customized by segment. For instance, you may want to have a pricing strategy against your monetize and grow quadrants, specifically internationals, rewards lover, and technocrats.

In short, your new insights based on the three pillars will help reveal drivers of your business. These are levers that you can pull to maximize ROI and drive the business forward. It plays both ways. Knowing how you want to grow your products or services will help determine how to interact with your customers. Knowing how your customers want to interact with you will determine what kind of services you might offer in the future. Your measurement framework is ultimately

EXHIBIT 8-6. Engage Your Customers

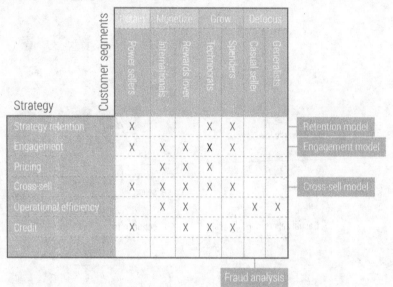

Strategy \ Customer segments	Retain	Monetize		Grow		Defocus	
	Power sellers	Internationals	Rewards lover	Technocrats	Spenders	Casual seller	Generalists
Strategy retention	X			X	X		
Engagement	X	X	X	X	X		
Pricing		X	X	X			
Cross-sell	X	X	X	X	X		
Operational efficiency		X	X			X	X
Credit	X		X	X	X		

Retention model — Engagement model — Cross-sell model

Fraud analysis

what ties these elements together and allows you to understand how you are working toward your company's strategies and priorities.

Executives high up in the organization already know their biggest KPIs, but the understanding of those KPIs becomes diluted as it travels down the organizational chart. This is counterproductive, as it is the understanding of drivers that finally uncovers the levers the business can pull to have impact on the KPIs. To effectively start leveraging data to make better decisions, all employees, irrespective of their business unit function, need to be trained to ask the right questions of data in their daily workflow so they will make the right decisions in their areas. This, ultimately, leads to the breakthrough insights needed to drive the KPIs and maximize ROI.

Do note that the answers to the 3 Key Questions will enable you to generate new insights as you dig deeper into your ever-changing business. This cannot happen overnight. It can take four to six weeks in a company with annual revenues of $100 million to $200 million, and three to four months for a company with annual revenues of $1 billion.

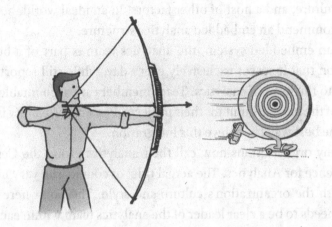

The understanding you have gained is not static. It can change as the business grows or changes, new trends from competition emerge, or industry landscape and technology shifts. People's engagement with smartphones now, for instance, has changed behavior on social media. The 3 Key Questions are, in essence, your tool to keep a constant eye on the continuously changing levers of your business so you can keep pulling the ones that look the most promising.

PART II: ORGANIZATIONAL STRUCTURE

Analytics performs a valuable function in the organization. It supports the critical decision making intended to bolster the organization's KPIs and impact the organization's balance sheet. Ultimately, analytics can play a key role in the company's success, particularly when it operates closely with the parts of the organization that can best leverage its output.

Team Structure

Every organization has its own take on organizational structure depending on the nature of the organization, its size, market, competition, culture, and a host of other factors. In an ideal world, however, we recommend an embedded analytics structure.

In an embedded system, the analytics team is part of a business function that it serves exclusively every day, while still reporting directly to the head of analytics. Team members are accountable to the head of the business unit for their projects. Physical proximity is probably the best way to achieve this integration.

Many organizations now call their analytics group the Center of Excellence for Analytics. The actual title, of course, can vary in keeping with the organization's culture and style. The point here is that there needs to be a clear leader of the analytics team within each business unit that has a P&L statement. The head of analytics reports directly to the CEO in a smaller organization (a $50,000 to $500,000 company) or to a general manager with a significant P&L charge in a larger organization (above $500 million in annual revenues) (see Exhibit 8-7).

EXHIBIT 8-7. Team Structure Model

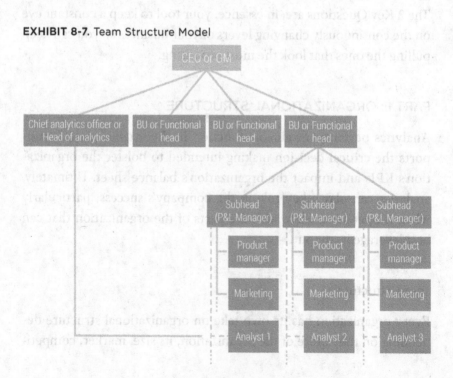

The core functions of the head of the analytics team are to:

1. Influence and manage the analytics agenda.
2. Build a data-driven culture—mentor and train analysts and enable training of business professionals.
3. Lay out a strategy of data infrastructure for productive use of analytics throughout the organization.

The head of analytics need not be your best analyst or a brilliant data scientist. Rather, the role is managerial, part visionary and part evangelist. Yes, the head of analytics should be a competent analyst, but more importantly he or she must be able to communicate the power of analytics to bolster its KPIs and increase the company's bottom line.

Team Composition

The actual team makeup is a function of the analytics agenda and the size and nature of the workload, but broadly speaking here is what we recommend (see Exhibit 8-8):

- In a company where business professionals do not yet have data-to-decisions skills, an analytics team could be made up of three business analysts, two data analysts, and one predictive analytics professional to support a team of 20 business professionals in marketing, product, operations, design, strategy, and other functions and verticals.
- In a company where business professionals already have data-to-decision skills, an analytics team may consist of a data analyst and a predictive analytics professional, who can support up to 20 business professionals.

In Chapter 9, we go deeper into the business track, where you will learn what you need to do at an individual level to drive impact through insights.

EXHIBIT 8-8. Team Composition

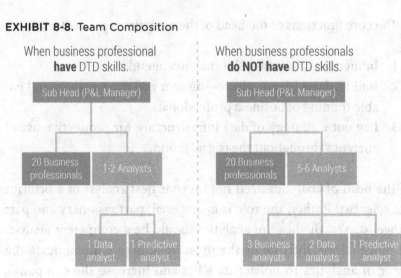

When business professional **have** DTD skills.

When business professionals **do NOT have** DTD skills.

IN A NUTSHELL

- You can follow a structured process like 3 Key Questions to formulate the analytics agenda.
- An embedded analytics structure is the most successful in delivering ROI to the organization.

NINE

Analytics Leader's Playbook

> **THIS CHAPTER WILL TALK ABOUT:**
>
> The first 90-day playbook for a business leader with new analytics responsibility.

Okay. You've gone this far; you have assessed your organization's analytics maturity, determined your analytics agenda, identified an appropriate organizational structure for the analytics initiative, and defined staffing, roles, and skills. So, how do you put it all in motion? Here is a playbook that would be particularly useful for the person who is newly appointed to head an analytics department. Here is what we recommend in two simple steps for setting up an analytics organization (see Exhibit 9-1).

EXHIBIT 9-1. The 90-Day Plan

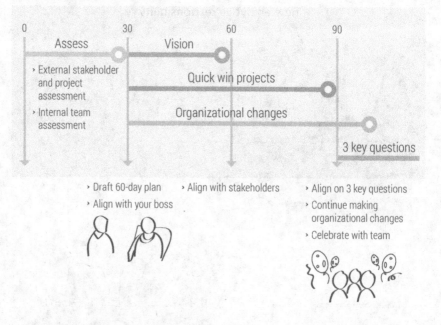

STEP 1: THE FIRST 30 DAYS: ASSESS

Ask your boss (CEO or GM) for 30 days to prepare an assessment of the organization before you come back with a plan.

I. High-Level External Assessment

1. Review past and current work, including the types of analytics projects that have been done in the last 12 months and their

business impact. This will give you a sense of the analytics competency and the appetite for analytics within your organization. It will also tell you whether your business partners are asking the right questions.

2. Talk to the leaders and business partners your team works with to understand their mindset. Ask about their key business questions, their analytics goals, and how they like to work with analytics teams. This will give you a sense of whether they regard your analytics team as a support function or as true business partner. It will illuminate the playing field and the path you have to follow to align with the stakeholders to succeed. In short, do an honest assessment of your organizational culture, with particular emphasis on readiness for analytics, adoption of data-to-decisions strategies, analytics maturity, and commitment of leadership and resources.

3. Finally, as you talk to the stakeholders identify some quick wins where your team can have meaningful business impact immediately and with little investment of time, resources, and funds. Start planting the seed for doing the 3 Key Questions exercise to identify the most impactful analytics agenda.

II. An Internal Team Assessment

1. Start with a skills assessment of your analytics team members. Of course as you look at analytical and data skills, don't forget to assess their soft skills as well.

2. Make sure to look at their past projects, the nature of their work, and how they use dashboards, simple analysis, or complex predictive analysis. This will help you assess the team's productivity, analytical ability, efficiency, and ability to drive impact.

3. Look at your team in terms of past focus areas, team dynamics, skills, and vendors used.

4. Review and assess your data infrastructure to ensure it is sufficient for the work you expect to take on.

5. Understand the current process used for prioritizing analytics projects (if one exists). If there isn't one, then you can plan to set one up.

STEP 2: THE NEXT 60 DAYS: PLAN AND EXECUTE

This 60-day plan is based on your assessment in Step 1. Discuss this with your manager to align priorities and resource allocation.

1. This discussion should include mission and goals for your team.
2. Lay out key projects with an estimate of required effort and resources by number, skills, and budget. These key projects are derived from the interviews with leaders of the organization that you did in your first 30 days.
3. Finally, create a management plan. This should estimate the amount of time you will spend on each focus area of your analytics strategy within the organization and what you will address in each area. Focus areas may cover the analytics agenda with current projects, as well as organizational changes, such as team structure, hiring and resource planning, training and coaching, and evangelizing data-driven culture.

Once the 60-day plan is executed and you have a few wins under your belt giving you credibility in the organization, it is time to follow the more formal 3 Key Questions approach to start informing your analytics agenda. As you execute against those, continue making the organizational changes—people, process, and tools—necessary to enable a more mature data-driven culture. Remember to align with stakeholders at regular intervals be it weekly, monthly, or quarterly. And make sure to celebrate successes with your team.

Making It Happen

THIS CHAPTER WILL TALK ABOUT:

How to truly drive impact in the organization.

The effective use of influencing, prioritization,
and coordination to amplify impact in the organization.

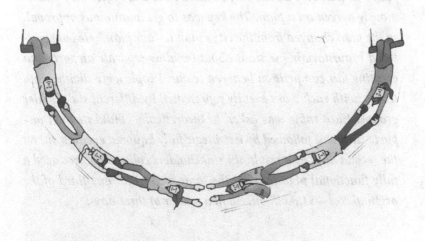

Bill Sherry was appointed Aviation Director of San Jose International Airport in 2005.[1] It was a terrible time for the airport, which was undergoing a much-needed $4.5 billion expansion that was putting undue financial pressure on all the key stakeholders, including the airline carriers and city council. Sherry came in and slashed the budget on this decade-old project by $3 billion. How? By aligning stakeholders with a common goal and providing an incentive for getting alignment. In September 2005, he locked a group of 48 stakeholders, including City Council members, airline executives, financial consultants, and engineers, in a conference room. They were given a common goal of agreeing on how to build the airport on a much smaller $1.5 billion budget. The incentive to agree on a plan was that they would only be allowed to leave after they unanimously agreed on a plan. The key was to get unanimous approval, so the plan changed from the city's plan to "our plan." He led structured brainstorming sessions about building separate airports and creating fair competition between teams. People were divided into teams, with each team evently represented by different stakeholder groups. Each table was asked to theoretically "build its own airport." This was followed by a strategic fully liquored evening out on the second day. As a result, the stakeholders collectively produced a fully functional plan to build the same airport for one-third of the original cost—$1.5 billion. All in a matter of three days!

Imagine the power and impact of the business track in aligning with all the stakeholders. And, not just in an airport, but in a company, the government, and social impact organizations. It can be a demanding and pressure-packed undertaking to lead projects that ultimately deliver results to drive the organization's growth. Often, as the product manager, marketing professional, operations manager, or analyst, you work under tight deadlines with limited resources. Yet, you are expected to come up with the right decisions and execute them seamlessly. Your initiatives are expected to bolster the target KPIs and add measurable business value. Of course, management wants the results right now.

For an analyst, performing the analysis well and coming up with the insights and recommendations should be enough. For a business professional, laying out a well-thought-through roadmap with quick insights to bolster your plan and executing against it should be enough, but it isn't.

The truth is that it takes more than just you to drive a decision into action so that it achieves business value. It requires alignment among key stakeholders—marketing managers, product managers, operations managers, and others on the front lines of the business. It requires alignment among the analyst who supports you with insights and data, your boss who is going to approve the budget if this action is taken, and perhaps his boss. Only if all these stakeholder are aware of and aligned with the decisions being made for the business can those decisions become actions for the organization. Ideally, you want your projects to have real impact throughout the organization.

To perform in a cross-functional environment and bring decisions to fruition, you would need to master some management techniques in addition to finding great actionable insights. Specifically, the skills that need grooming are influencing, prioritization, and coordination.

INFLUENCING

In a cross-functional organization, your ability to influence starts by recognizing these basic principles:

- Making decisions collaboratively and leveraging others' domain expertise is more effective than making decisions as an individual.
- Engaging stakeholders from the start will accelerate execution, whether they are your execution partners or budget approvers.

Whether the project involves building a better product or experience for your customers, improving the marketing campaign to drive engagement, or saving costs in operations, analytics can play an important role, possibly the critical role, in achieving your goals in the most accelerated fashion. Although achieving goals is often not a function of your individual expertise, but rather that of your team, you are part of a cross-functional project, either as a contributor or a leader. Therefore, there is an advantage in bringing everyone on board together to work enthusiastically and effectively across functions.

Whether it is website changes to improve customer engagement, improving the patient experience during emergency check-in at a hospital, or reducing the cost of goods for a manufacturing unit, you need to influence your cross-functional team to drive cohesively to the same vision and goal you are tasked with.

Boosting your influence starts with building alignment with stakeholders at the outset of an initiative. There are four stages of any initiative or project (see Exhibit 10-1):

1. **Vision:** Define "that" which you want to drive the team toward.
2. **Plan:** Lay out a plan detailing scope, stakeholders, resources, and timelines.
3. **Execute:** Act according to the plan, and adjust it in flight if required.
4. **Learn:** Learn from this initiative and feed the results into your next project.

EXHIBIT 10-1. How to Use Your Influence

Take time to socialize success and learnings.

4. Learn

1. Vision

Influencing starts early. Engage stakeholders in ideation. Formulate a common vision which motivates and aligns with different groups.

Run tight project plans. Enable transparent, regular communication of progress, plan, and problem solve. Hold people to action items.

3. Execute

2. Plan

Get inputs from different groups for formulating plan of action, socialize widely, and get buy-in from all stakeholders, including commitment for resources.

Vision

Influencing starts early with building consensus around the vision. The key is to formulate a common vision that will motivate and align with the objectives of different groups. Some quick tips to achieving this goal are:

- If groups are fairly misaligned, build consensus one on one.
- Remember, no idea is a bad idea in the ideation stage.
- Have a sponsor who can champion the initiative before going in.

Planning

When formulating the plan of action, it helps to get input from all involved groups. Once the plan is finalized, socialize widely with all the stakeholders to get buy-in. You not only need to get buy-in on your approach and timelines, but you also need commitments for the resources required. A quick tip is to get formal and written commitment from stakeholders on resources approved for the plan, and their roles.

Execution

Running a tight ship is key to successful execution. You need to manage project timelines that include a plan for regular communication of progress and for resolving any roadblocks that might arise. It will be critical to hold people accountable to the action items and timelines assigned.

A quick tip is to communicate effectively. Include all stakeholders in periodic update emails. Attendance of all stakeholders not directly responsible for execution should be optional at meetings. The updates should be brief and action oriented to help everyone keep track of the developments, particularly when they are not involved in day-to-day activities.

Learning

Finally, when the initiative is a success, learn from it. You and the team should celebrate! Ensure you generously spread the credit and involve all the stakeholders in the celebration. This is the best time to share your success and what you have learned. This will help other groups in the organization learn new things about customers and the products in a way that could serve as input for their respective projects. A quick tip is to give credit to all the participants and take the time to celebrate.

PRIORITIZATION

Don't we all wish we had 40 hours every day to catch up on our long to-do list? And, at work, don't we have more to do than we could finish in a lifetime? Multiply that by the number of people in your execution team and the need to prioritize becomes clear. Prioritization is the process of aligning limited resources with highest impact initiatives to drive toward the organization's vision and goals. Prioritization is a very important process to effectively manage any type of organization, business unit, or function.

Prioritization in its simplest form involves understanding the investment (I) and returns (R) from each initiative and ranking the initiatives with best ROI or highest R. The problem is that initiatives do not come with R and I attached to them. They are usually great ideas that are coming from different groups. There are many initiatives that have no direct financial goals; they are done for other reasons, such as improving stakeholder value or improving brand perception.

Prioritization is tricky and we recommend the following standardized four-step process:

1. **Form a core team with representation from different groups working on the initiative.** For example, if you are a head of product marketing group, create a small leadership team for prioritization, which involves people in your team, as well as people from product development, analytics, and any other group that is involved in the delivery of your projects. Without this democratic decision-making process involving stakeholders from different groups, there is risk of animosity and perceived conflict of interest, which could be counterproductive.

2. **Agree on prioritization metrics and criteria.** The first step is for all stakeholders to agree on the criteria for prioritization and be sure they align with the organization's goals and priorities. The sizing and estimation methodology could help estimate the impact of the project on such factors as expected revenue, ROI, or reduction in churn. In addition to prioritization criteria, you can establish criteria to filter out requests. Common filtration metrics include strategic alignment (e.g., This is a great project, but it doesn't align with our overall positioning); actionability (e.g., Can we do it?); availability of data (e.g., Do we have good and easily accessible data?); minimum ROI (e.g., What is the minimum expected returns for investment?); maximum investment (e.g., We won't do any project which requires more than 20 product development days). Whatever you do, agree on criteria for prioritization and filtration before you start applying them to projects. This will confirm that your approach is fair and transparent.

3. **Establish a process for accepting new ideas and then meet regularly and frequently to prioritize them.** Prioritization is

a process that should be performed by the group at regularly scheduled meetings. It is also important to create a transparent process by which new ideas and innovation can foster. The more fleshed out these project ideas are, the easier it is to prioritize them.

4. **Adjust priorities based on new inputs.** As a result of these meetings, both the process of prioritization and the prioritization criteria will evolve. Be prepared, and be flexible.

COORDINATION

When working in a large organization with many business units (BU), formal and structured coordination will help align functional groups and BUs to orchestrate activity across teams and reduce redundancy to make the biggest impact. To help with coordination, always start by defining a common learning agenda and have regular meetings or brown bag lunches to share roadmaps and knowledge. This will ensure that all groups are on the same page. It also helps you avoid overlapping efforts, which are wasteful and frustrating. Finally, prepare a weekly or monthly communication—usually an email is sufficient—to

update everyone on what is happening. We also find it helpful to informally reach out to different groups in the organization to learn who may be working on which other projects.

The steps above will surely help you generate significant impact through your work, whichever part of the organization you serve. The next chapter looks at common pitfalls in business analytics.

IN A NUTSHELL

- Effective influencing can help accelerate the execution of any initiative.
- Prioritization is a necessary process, which, when done democratically can foster innovation while keeping the organization focused on the big rocks.
- Coordination across groups can save on redundancy and create a harmonious organization in which teams build on each other's success.

ELEVEN

Common Pitfalls

THIS CHAPTER WILL TALK ABOUT:

What critical mistakes you as business leader, analytics leader, business user, or analyst are likely to make.

How to avoid making those mistakes.

It is day two on the job. A young Jay was asked to lead a conversion modeling project. His employer, a young and newly global technology company, had only a new global technology group and had yet to evolve an analytics-based decision-making culture. This project was unusually complex, as it involved hundreds of variables, and too complex to throw to a new person on his second day on the job. He barely knew where the men's room was.

With pressure to complete the project quickly and successfully, Jay missed one of the most important lessons we teach—getting alignment with all the key stakeholders. He aligned himself with one senior leader's vision, but he didn't invest in getting buy-in from other stakeholders. He even skipped touching base with the product manager, who would actually be responsible for acting on any findings Jay's team came up with.

Jay and his team wrestled with the mind-boggling complexity of their model for two months. They produced an excellent conversion model that pointed out five major variables driving conversion. He then presented the findings to a wider audience, including the senior leader he initially conferred with, senior product leaders, and the product manager in charge of that particular product. They had merely glanced at the executive summary before remarking, "Um. We already know these factors drive conversion from our other research." Jay realized his mistake. The meeting went downhill from that point, with Jay scrambling to defend his team's work while emphasizing the few new insights they did come up with. A dynamic, however, had been established at that moment: product team versus analytics. It took six months to build trust with the product team. And even then he succeeded only by consistently and repeatedly delivering fresh insights.

Everyone makes a mistake sooner or later. You will too. The idea is to learn from these mistakes.

It is to avoid mistakes such as Jay's that an integral part of the BADIR framework is to ask the right questions and touch base with the stakeholders. This is not a trivial step to skip to save time. We know how important it is and how easy it is to overlook.

Let's discuss the four categories of users involved in analytics and the common mistakes they make. Simply being aware of these mistakes should go far in helping you to avoid them. The four categories of users are business leader, business manager, analytics leader, and analyst. This chapter offers a cheat sheet of common pitfalls for each of these roles, as it is very important to recognize and thereby avoid them.

BUSINESS LEADER: PITFALLS

1. **Not knowing how to measure success for your organization.** As a business leader you need to be clear on the key outcomes you want to deliver and how to measure success for achieving them. Without that clarity, you will not be able to  really leverage data and analytics to the advantage of the business. More important, without success metrics to show, you will not be able to convince other business managers and corporate executives of the value of your data-enabled decisions. You should start by using KPIs to measure key outcomes, ensuring that the KPIs are aligned with the organization's objectives.

2. **Not knowing the drivers of success and aligning projects to those drivers.** This goes one step deeper than understanding the KPIs. Only by knowing the drivers of the KPIs can you align projects with them to accomplish the desired business outcomes. Start by initiating analytics to understand what drives the KPIs, and then set up a process to review what projects are aligned against these drivers by using an approach like 3 Key Questions. This will help you identify new project opportunities and adjust the priorities of existing projects in

the pipeline. For most of our clients who started using the 3 Key Questions framework, we found that 50 percent of their projects require readjustments in priorities and a significant number get defunded once this process emphasizes the "pullable levers" that move the business.

3. **Lacking a data-enabled, decision-making culture.** Few organizations start with a data-enabled culture. It has to first be championed, then demonstrated to work, and finally cultivated and nurtured. So business leaders who want to be data driven are the key to a data-enabled culture. There is a method to this madness, and leaders can accelerate this process by:

- Attributing decisions to the decision makers and holding them accountable for the outcome, whether good or bad. Otherwise, people never look back and learn.
- Fostering a clear and transparent decision-making process, as opposed to making dictatorial decisions.
- Hiring a strong leader of analytics and granting that person extensive latitude to set the analytics agenda, rather than engaging task executers.
- Creating a mechanism to listen and respond to your customers and to design great solutions and experiences. Without this mechanism, your business is not customer driven.
- Investing in a data and analytics infrastructure appropriately, as opposed to developing a spontaneous patched-up information architecture that seldom enables easy and quick access to relevant data.

4. **Engaging in gut-based decision making.** A dictatorial decision-making process is typically one in which decisions are made based solely on someone's intuition about a business problem or solution. Is your allegiance to analytics limited to encouraging analysts to try to prove what your leadership team has already decided or wants to be proved? What happens if the data does not support your answer or if it completely contradicts the favored answer? A business can compete on data only if leaders keep open and flexible minds, provide strongest held

beliefs as hypotheses, and are willing to change direction if the data contradicts those hypotheses.

5. **Throwing the data scientist at the data to find insights.** Throwing 10 data scientists at a company's database to build complex models will not yield the insights to drive the business unless the leader first understands the problem that needs to be solved using the data. By asking probing questions that are aligned to the business drivers and supporting the data scientists with informed hypotheses, the analysis will deliver fresh actionable insights from the data.

6. **Treating analytics as a cost center rather than a profit center.** Often, only profit centers get a seat at the management table. If you are a GM or a CEO, you probably have all the functional heads, such as marketing and product development, on your leadership team. If you are a head of such a function, you would have the heads of all the subgroups as your decision-making team. If analytics is considered a costly support function within an organization, the head of analytics may not find a seat at the table and, consequently, is downstream of decisions. This is often because the impact of insights from analytics is not directly attributed to the analytics team. A $2 million growth or cost savings insight is attributed entirely to the function that implements the strategy, while analytics is seen as a support function.

   Here we would like to highlight a great opportunity that is lost when analytics does not have that seat at the decision-makers' table. For one thing, it diminishes the perception of analytics as a valuable contributor and profit driver. It signals to others in your organization that analytics is a use-if-needed function. Second, it excludes analytics from the context of the business—from gaining a deep understanding of the business and providing input based on what is learned from analyzing the data. Analytics output is only as powerful as the business context the analyst is aware of. Third, and most important, analytics can only half serve the business if it does not contribute to making decisions. At the executive table, an analytics head can contribute objectively from prior insights about the business and current business trends to decide which early hypotheses to support, all without being burdened by downstream P&L choices. This is where analytics reaches a higher strategic level within an organization, supporting groundbreaking innovation as well as incremental decisions to deliver P&L goals.

To truly leverage your investment in analytics, start by giving analytics a seat and voice at the management table, so analysts can be immersed in the context and bring about transformational ideas from the depths of their insights.

7. **Not embedding analytics close to P&L.** The most effective analytics teams are embedded within business groups at the appropriate P&L size. This allows team members to know the business from the inside and be true partners of the business group. A centralized analytics group, on the other hand, may not appreciate business priorities or understand the business nearly as well as embedded analytics teams. A centralized analytics group could also fall into a trap of fielding requests from multiple groups and using a haphazard mechanism to prioritize requests without understanding potential business impact. However, a centralized group can drive impact if it is still set up as a matrix organization moving the analyst closer to the business context.

8. **Conflicting analytics teams.** Whichever way analytics resources are organized within your company, there may be multiple analytics teams for different verticals. This is good if it enables the team to tackle more questions and assist with more localized decisions. However, team conflicts can occur when a business group assigns the same analytics problem to multiple teams due to a lack of confidence in one team or because group members are shopping for an answer that reinforces their preconceived answer. In either case, this not only undermines analytics resources but also creates a culture

of distrust, which leads to wasted resources, damaged employee motivation, and the possibility that the best talent will leave the organization. So, best practice is to limit one assignment to one analytics team based on the BU or function the team is part of. If lack of confidence in a team is an issue, it needs to be addressed independently.

9. **Not fully understanding the power of analytics.** As a business leader, you need to be aware of the potential of analytics and particularly what it can do for your business. Otherwise, your leadership team might not value and support analytics to drive impact in the organization. We have seen that some leaders may have had an anemic experience with analytics, as, for instance, in trying to resolve a potentially low-impact problem that yielded a low-impact response from analytics. Similarly, some leaders may have seen little benefit of analytics groups and not felt the need to hire a senior analytics leader. This can lead to a vicious cycle where current analysis resources do not have the capability to deliver high-impact analytics projects, which leads managers to not invest in effective analytics and therefore never get high-impact results.

For most of our clients who are early in their journey to become data driven, we start with an executive workshop to showcase the power of analytics: What is it, how is it done, and how other organization have used it effectively. This should inspire leaders into action toward setting up a data-driven culture.

10. **Outsourcing analytics.** A data-driven organization is internally equipped with systems to learn about its customers and how they use their products. It then leverages these insights to make future products that delight customers. In our experience as in-house analytics leaders, we have seen that external consultants often postulate some misleading insights or are simply not adding value. This is because they don't have the business context or the time to immerse themselves in a company's nuanced internal data. Even as external consultants ourselves, we still maintain that hiring external consultants to deliver day-to-day insights is not a scalable, long-term solution. A well-supported internal analytics team brings a deep knowledge of the data, along with the business context, and is better prepared to pose and answer hypotheses relevant to the business. Overreliance on external consultants also signals to your internal resources that you do not trust their capabilities, which, needless to say, does not help morale.

However, external consultants can be beneficially leveraged to accelerate the journey for a company to be become data driven. They can provide a valuable outside-in view and use their expertise to help set up methods and processes for an organization to be truly data driven. External consultants can also be used to support your internal team.

For a summary of these pitfalls, see Exhibit 11-1.

EXHIBIT 11-1. Keys to Success as a Business Leader in a Data-Driven Company

Define the measure of success for your organization.
Uncover the drivers of your business, and align your internal projects to those drivers.
Build a data-enabled, decision-making culture.
Inculcate data-based decision making within your team.
Ask good, high-impact questions of the data instead of throwing analytics resources on to data.
Give analytics a seat at the table; hire the right head of analytics.
Embed analytics resources within the businesses they need to optimize.
Don't ask the same question of three different analytics teams.
Insource analytics by developing internal capabilities—people, processes, and tools.

BUSINESS MANAGER: PITFALLS

1. **Giving only lip-service to data-driven decision making.** With Big Data all the rage, a business manager would seem behind the times if he or she didn't use data to drive decisions. Still, if you only really want to use analytics as a tool to propagate a preestablished agenda and ignore insights from data that dispute that agenda, then it really is of no benefit. With more and more business leaders insisting on data-driven decision making, it is a prudent career decision for a business manager to develop a sincere appreciation for its power. This will preclude you from making gut-based decisions that turn out to be deficient or have no valid data or methodology to back up recommended actions.

2. **Depending on other people for insights.** As analytics is better integrated into a business and responds to an increased demand for insights, it might be more efficient and more effective for business managers to rely on themselves for insights using simple analysis. The benefit is that you receive good and early

insights without waiting for an analytics team to prioritize the request. With training in simple analysis using Excel, you can proactively hypothesize and glean insights from readily available data. This would, in turn, help engage the analytics team more effectively to either validate hypotheses and insights gained from these simple analytics or develop more complex solutions for complex questions.

3. **Trying to measure everything.** You've seen them, maybe even contributed to them—the dashboards with 300 metrics. In one of our projects, at an instrumentation meeting, the product owner proposed close to 500 metrics to be instrumented and reported on a daily basis. Okay, it's good to instrument key metrics in case you need a deep dive, but no one can or should read through a 500-metric report every day. You don't want to pay your people to do that.

A business manager should drive the team to think in terms of two to three key success metrics and 20 to 30 drivers of these key metrics. This not only focuses the business on the things that actually move the needle, but it also makes it possible to build a decision-enabling report in weeks instead of months. The big benefit, though, is that it forces teams and leaders to

think more deeply about the top 30 highly visible metrics with which to run the business.

4. **Not knowing what questions to ask.** To paraphrase a popular expression: "Good questions in, good insights out." You should start analytics with asking good questions based on your knowledge of the business. This applies to business managers as much as it does to analysts. Managers in narrow silos may not even know what business questions to ask or what analytics is capable of doing. It is less a crystal ball and more a powerful business tool you can use and shape. To gain a perspective on the potential of analytics as a tool, you will benefit from learning about analytics through reading, attending conferences, and interactions with experts who have leveraged analytics for impact. The goal is to familiarize yourself with analytics so you ask the kind of questions that will lead to good insights. Refer to the 3 Key Questions framework in Chapter 8. Another way of looking at "what questions to ask" is to think about which questions will result in insights you can put to work to deliver business impact. There is a difference between questions that produce information that may be nice to know and questions whose answers provide need-to-have insights. The nice-to-know questions will satisfy someone's curiosity or may seem intriguing, but the answers will not lead to any change in the business. When the questions lead to impactful insights, your organization should have the willingness to change. If the willingness to act isn't there or if the potential impact from the changes is low, you will only be wasting your scarce analytics resources.

5. **Not prioritizing.** Once you have a list of 20 questions, it seems logical to let your team approach them one at a time, but this is an extravagant luxury of time that many companies can no longer afford, particularly as business now moves so quickly. Analyzing 20 questions will take time and resources that can better be used elsewhere. You would be better off taking a little more time to prioritize those 20 questions using a business filter and then fashion them down to the top three to five that

have the best chance of delivering business value. Of the remaining ideas, set aside the next three to five with the greatest potential impact for a second phase, if the resources are still available.

6. **Believing you don't have enough clean data to get insights.** We hear this from our clients all the time. While in rare cases you really may not have any clean data, this is not true for most companies. Rather than be cowed into a state of inaction because you think you don't have data, just ask your key questions and let your team work through what data is actually required to answer them. You and your team will be surprised how far you can go with the data you actually have. A well-documented, credible answer is better than no answer. One client, for example, asked us to come up with an estimate of the lifetime value of a customer. The client didn't have much data, but some was available. We set up the system to capture six months worth of new and clean data to estimate repeat behavior and get lifetime value, which we then projected out to one-year and two-year values. It was enough to get the company going in the right direction.

7. **Expecting data to tell the answers.** This is the corollary to starting analytics with the right questions and hypotheses, not

with the data. Data doesn't speak; it responds. Just asking the analyst to come back with "all the relevant data" won't do much to advance the business strategy or objective.

Not only is this very time-consuming but it is also very frustrating for your analytics team. It will also propagate the perception that you do not know the drivers of your business. In short, data is just data; using it to prove or disprove hypotheses is how it delivers value.

8. **Believing too much in the latest buzzwords.** For many, predictive analytics, Big Data, and machine learning are the hot stuff in data-driven management. They are truly that—buzzwords. While it is good to learn about them, know that these concepts are costly overkill for most of the problems you are trying to resolve and probably do not address your immediate business needs. In the end, effective data-driven decision making still comes down to asking the right business questions and having the hypotheses to address them using business analytics. After this, if you still need predictive analytics to help solve the business need, it will be a well-defined scope thanks to your initial quick analysis.

9. **Viewing analytics as rocket science, brain surgery, or magic.** Maybe it is the predictive nature of some advanced analytics that makes business managers swoon. Predictive analytics is a science and a structured discipline; it is not magic. In Chapter 4, we discussed the commonly used analytics methodologies. Familiarize yourself with both the possibilities and the limitations of them all. Then, you can discuss analytics without being intimidated and know enough to ask your team to deliver on all types of analyses appropriate to your issues without being swayed by magic or rocket science.

For a summary of these pitfalls, see Exhibit 11-2.

EXHIBIT 11-2. Keys to Success as a Business Manager Using Analytics Insight

Make decisions based on data; you will consistently drive results if you do.
Learn analytics; nobody keeps money in a neighbor's house, why should you?
Find the top 20 metrics you want to run your business with, and operationalize them.
Learn what question to ask your data using 3 Key Questions.
Constantly prioritize your analytics, as well as your projects.
Leverage the data you already have before fretting about what you don't have.
Don't expect data to reveal insights; instead, ask the right questions to uncover the insights.
Don't get distracted by the latest buzzwords, and keep an eye on your top 20 metrics.

ANALYTICS LEADER: PITFALLS

1. **Not having an executive sponsor.** For an organization that does not have analytics in its DNA, the journey to becoming data driven is a change management process, and not an easy overnight turnaround. Someone with executive powers in the organization needs to champion the analytics-driven decision making. Without that, it is impossible for an analytics leader to have significant impact in the organization. As an analytics leader, you need executive sponsorship to get inputs on direction of the organization. You also need the blessing of a senior sponsor to have the permission to question the status quo and bring about changes in decision-making processes, organizational structure, and infrastructure to leverage analytics for decision making. Someday analytics will have a seat at the C-level table. Until then, you need an executive champion.

2. **Not aligning with business goals.** One of our CEO friends was extremely disappointed with analytics. Not people who let such a feeling (about analytics) slide, we discovered that he had hired

a chief data scientist about 18 months prior with great hopes of getting on the Big Data bandwagon. The chief then hired a team of 12 statisticians and started solving complex problems with advanced and complex algorithms. As expected, those problems took long to solve, but unfortunately did not quite move the business. The CEO, a year and a couple of million dollars later, was disappointed with his analytics investment. Under pressure from the board, he fired the chief and his team. As it turned out, the chief data scientist was entirely motivated by technology and not driven by business outcome. Working on analytical research projects is intellectually rewarding. But outside of academia, analytics work should be aligned with real and important business goals. Without such alignment, you will not have consistent support for analytics. And, without that support, you will find projects being stopped midstream (as when, for example, there is a disappointing quarterly report and someone wants to cut costs). In other cases, you may be able to complete the analysis project but not get the resources to see your recommendations implemented. And, until recommendations are implemented, the organization gets no value from the analytics. When aligned with business goals, analytics can become an indispensable key to the success of a business.

3. **Taking a reactive rather than a transformational approach to the analytics agenda.** If analytics leaders do not ask for a seat at the management table, it is quite likely they will not become aware of strategic ideas or initiatives under consideration. Without knowing that, you will not be able to influence the direction of the organization. You and your team will simply be reactive, taking directives from senior management. You could, instead, capitalize on your position to proactively come up with initiatives. Leverage your special position of knowing your customers through their data and data trends. Align with executive leadership on the direction of the company, as well as gaps in understanding by using a framework, such as the 3 Key Questions. Instead of your work becoming a sequence of short-lived

reactive projects with, at best, tactical value, it should deliver a real payoff based on analytical, strategic, and transformational insights.

4. **Thinking small.** An analytics leader's role can be as big as he or she wants it to be. However, you can easily get distracted by supporting small-to-medium impact projects—collecting a series of wins with minimal impact. Good analytics leaders have to think big and become involved in the strategic discussion. You can't wait to be invited in; you must make your way into the discussion on the strength of your big thinking (which is why you need an executive champion behind you). Using a structured approach like the 3 Key Questions, you can focus the organization on the strategic priorities, align the internal projects to those priorities, and contribute with instantly actionable insights to drive massive impact.

5. **Not building cross-functional alignment between business and analytics.** This often results in multiple analytics teams working on the same problem for different groups. Such misalignment with business groups often leads to conflict with leaders who begin questioning the value your group is adding. The hope is to minimize such conflicts and replace them by working efficiently as true partners.

6. **Not building the right team.** You can't do it all alone, and you are only as good as your team. That is why you have to hire people with the right combination of analytic and communications skills, technical competencies, and leadership ability. You want a mix of business analytics, advanced analytics, and data skills. You would also want to look for people who relish solving puzzles and bring a can-do, take-charge attitude to the project. Few people walk in the door with all these diverse talents, so find people who have the basic skills and can be groomed for the rest. Remember that you will have to pick up the slack.

7. **Not continuously cultivating and motivating the team.** Sometimes analytics work can be frustrating. Sometimes the pressure

and tight deadlines can be grueling. Sometimes dealing with the stakeholders can have your people pulling out their hair. Nothing demotivates analysts faster than knowing that they worked overtime and used their brain cells to answer a nice-to-know question with no real consequence. Additionally, people on your team need to feel they are growing professionally and becoming more marketable. To that end you need to make sure:

- Your team is working on the right problems with best bet to drive impact.
- You are generous with praise when earned.
- You are empathetic when things hit a rocky patch.
- You are ready to motivate and incentivize when spirits lag.
- You are attentive to opportunities for team members to learn, attend conferences, and gain professional recognition.

Yes, you run the risk of some rock stars being wooed away, but people who are doing satisfying work, driving significant impact, enjoying recognition and appreciation, receiving opportunities to learn and develop, and are being competitively paid will stick with the leader who shows he or she has their interests at heart.

8. **Not having input into the data infrastructure.** If you are not involved in the instrumentation and infrastructure planning discussions, you, your team, and your business counterparts will be held back by the quality of the data and the speed at which they can access it. Therefore, it is important for you to participate in the planning, architecture, and design of data infrastructure, such as servers and BI tools. You don't have to become an IT person, but you do want to provide input in the process so the right tradeoffs are made to enable your team and the business teams to access data easily. Remember, if it isn't easy to use, it won't be used.

9. **Building an empire versus delivering business value.** If you invest first in hiring people and building a huge team, sooner or later an executive will question the value you are adding. Our experience indicates that it is better to deliver excellent results

for the business with a smaller team before requesting an increased budget that will enable you to add people. Excellent business results attract more projects, which will give you the opportunity to build your team without forcing it. Your champions will be demanding a bigger team for you on your behalf.

For a summary of these pitfalls, see Exhibit 11-3.

EXHIBIT 11-3. Keys to Success as an Analytics Leader

Have an executive sponsor; it might be your manager.
Align your internal resources and time to your true North—the business goals.
Use the 3 Key Questions to drive an analytics agenda with biggest potential to drive results.
Think big—what metric can you move with the resources you currently have?
Build cross-functional alignment across analytics and business functions.
Build the right team driven by the analytics agenda.
Cultivate and motivate your team; inspired team members will go beyond their mandate to deliver.
Provide input to the data infrastructure to make data access easy for your team, as well as your business counterparts.
Focus on delivering business value, and not on empire building.

ANALYST: PITFALLS

1. **Not aligning with stakeholders.** You must align with the key stakeholders from the start of the project. Otherwise, you could miss the opportunity to leverage their insights and find yourself reinventing the wheel. So yes, check-in with all the stakeholders at the start of the project and check back with them multiple times during the project. Be sure to update them on your findings as you proceed. No one likes surprises, so give them regular information on where your team is headed. Certainly, do this before you make a final presentation. Otherwise, it may

be you who gets the biggest surprise. Beyond strained personal relations, alienating key stakeholders can pave the way for road-blocks to implementing your best insights and recommenda-tions and a lack of support for the business impact you hoped to achieve. Sounds ominous, but it is so simple to resolve.

2. **Failing to identify key stakeholders.** The main stakeholders are usually obvious—product manager, CMO, VP of Sales—but there may be others who are less obvious although they also play an important role. This could be the VP of Operations, the Head of Compliance, or maybe even the CFO. The point here is to not miss any, as Jay did in the case study at the beginning of this chapter. BADIR recommends that to avoid missing any stakeholders, ask who will take action, who needs to give per-mission, and who will approve the budget.

3. **Not knowing the real business question.** The manager who gives you the brief on an analytics project may not have di-vulged the whole story in that brief, despite best intentions. Without spending the time it takes to uncover and understand the real and underlying business question and the background to it, you run the risk of not addressing the real issue the man-ager wants your team to resolve. That's why you have to probe. This is how you can achieve serious impact with analytics. Iron-ically, your manager may be satisfied with the insights you bring back even if they don't drive any decisions or have any impact, but you shouldn't be.

4. **Not defining the measure of success for your project.** How can you determine if you have achieved your objective without knowing what defines success for your project? You need the right yardstick for the particular objective, as well as a specific goal. Does success mean an increase in the conversion rate of first-time customers or an increase in revenue from existing customers? Either will increase revenue, but if the business ex-pects to increase the number of new customers then increasing revenue from existing customers, nice as it is, won't be consid-ered a success. The way to avoid arguments about success is to

define the project's success metrics, its yardstick, and the specific goal or number you want to achieve in the analytics plan. You do this by asking a few key questions:

- What is our specific success metric (e.g., revenue, customer growth, reduced churn)?
- What is our criteria for success (e.g., 5 percent increase in revenue or surpassing a particular benchmark)?
- Have we created instrumentation to measure the right metrics (e.g., Are we collecting the data needed to determine that success)?

5. **Starting with the data.** It seems natural to start analytics with the data since that is what you are analyzing, but this would be a big mistake. Remember our discussion in Chapter 2 about explorers and detectives? It is too easy to get lost in the vast sea of data that even small companies face. Start with a clarified business question, and navigate using hypotheses. As discussed in Chapter 4, the hypotheses will keep you focused on where you should be looking and what data you should be looking for. If you start with data rather than a hypothesis, you are likely to miss some key variable or blow the budget or the schedule, or both.

6. **Not having a plan for analysis.** Having a plan is a key part of managing expectations. The plan lays out the scope of the analysis project, the resources available, and the timeframe. It presents an opportunity to align all the stakeholders with the plan. Without an analysis plan, you are vulnerable to any manager's newly implied or stated expectations. A plan will clearly show whether or not such requests can be accommodated, and if there's a cost and resource impact. A plan lets you know how many and what resources you would need. Of course, if the manager with high expectations has the clout to free up additional resources (people, technology, budget, or time), you can always talk to them about expanding the plan to possibly encompass the new expectations.

7. **Using the incorrect methodology.** Familiarize yourself with the methodologies you can apply. Know their strengths and

shortcomings, where they work best, and when and how you can effectively deploy them. Choosing the wrong methodology can undermine your best efforts. The solution is simple: Get a strong grounding in the fundamentals from the outset. Know your methodologies.

8. **Not customizing your analytics presentation for the particular audience.** You want to aim your presentation at the particular audience you are addressing. Business executives, for example, need a different level of detail than operations people. If you delve into details with an audience made up of senior business leaders, you could possibly lose them in the first five minutes. Senior business leaders typically prefer to get the bigger picture—insights, impact, recommendations—before digging into details. Of course, there always are exceptions. So, knowing your audience and customizing your presentation specifically to its members can make your presentation a success. Yes, it means a little more work, but it is better than the alternative, which is having them cut you off or walk out in the middle (or nod off). None of these does wonders for your work.

For a summary of these pitfalls, see Exhibit 11-4.

EXHIBIT 11-4. Keys to Success as an Analyst

Identify and align with all the stakeholders.
Take the time to understand the real business question before starting to dig for insights.
Take the time to customize your presentation for its intended audience.
If you want powerful actionable insights, don't start with data.
Always have a written analysis plan, even if it is only a half-page document.
Take time to identify the methodology you will use, and spell it out in the analysis plan.
Define measures of success for your project.

Awareness of these common mistakes is often enough to avoid them. In other cases, the solution involves simple, basic best management practices and familiarity with analytics. Good luck.

IN A NUTSHELL

- If you are a business leader, define your measures of success, uncover drivers of those success metrics, and orient your entire team toward them.
- If you are a business manager, ask the right questions of data and learn to do simple analytics.
- If you are an analytics leader, lay out an analytics agenda aligned to the success metrics and make data access easy across the organization.
- If you are an analyst, align with the key stakeholders and use the BADIR framework to solve any business problem with data.

4

ANALYTICS AT WORK

Ten Case Studies

This section is designed to illustrate a few applications of business and advanced analytics in diverse industries, from schools to sports to health. We hope these will inspire and fuel your creative thinking to solve business challenges with an analytical framework and a smart mix of tools.

Case Study 1: Back to Power

Situation: For President Barack Obama, reelection was not a certainty. Facing significant political challenges, the race was going to be close and tough. His two broadest challenges were to raise adequate campaign funds and to convince Americans he was the right person for the job.

Actions: Obama for America (OFA) maximized every best practice in analytics, surveying, testing, visualizing, and reporting to formulate a data-driven strategic framework. Over 50 data analysts worked through voter data to predict the individual behavior of millions of Americans.

His team had three simple goals—get everyone who voted the first time to vote again, bring in new voters from new growing demographics, and sway undecided voters through targeted messaging.

Microtargeting Models: Obama's team used data from numerous surveys, interaction with voters, volunteers, donors, and website users, and a 180-million-person voter file to build several microtargeting models to assess two factors: Would the voter cast a ballot, and would the voter support Obama? By estimating support for Obama versus Romney in each state and media market, the campaign calculated Obama's chances of winning each state. Models were adjusted weekly, and the data informed the "Get Out the Vote" and persuasion campaigns to vote for Obama.

Communication Analytics: OFA had a tool to review speeches in local newspapers to determine which parts were quoted most often and what people's reactions were across geographic regions. Speechwriters tracked which messages were being covered and whether they were in line with the messages the campaign wanted to convey to the voters.

The campaign's strategy to crowd source funds was powered by analytics and had the positive consequence of engaging voters.

Testing: A/B tests were done extensively. Fundraising emails were tested to identify those with the best response rates. In one effort, the OFA tested 18 variations of the subject line and email copy. The winning variation, "I will be outspent," raised more than $2.6 million. The website was optimized by conducting 240 A/B tests on the donation page, resulting in a 49 percent increase in conversion rate.

Response Analytics and Targeted Communications: Instead of asking for a fixed contribution amount, the campaign tested different percentages of donors' highest previous amounts and found that those messages were more successful in raising funds. Strategies based on recipients' past responses to email campaigns helped better target communication. For example, recipients were targeted based on whether they had donated online or volunteered in the past.

Impact: We are all aware of the results of the campaign. What many might not be aware of is that the models predicted the outcomes within a very small margin of error, a range of +/−2.5 percent. OFA's final projection was a 51 to 48 battleground-state margin for the president, which is approximately where the race ended up. Analytics was able to make a national campaign as targeted as a local city council campaign.

References

www.technologyreview.com/featuredstory/509026/how-obamas-team-used
   -big-data-to-rally-voters/
engagedc.com/download/Inside%20the%20Cave.pdf
techpresident.com/news/23214/how-analytics-made-obamas-campaign
   -communications-more-efficient
http://www.businessweek.com/articles/2012-11-29/the-science-behind
   -those-obama-campaign-e-mails

Case Study 2: Winning the Olympics

Situation: The United States had not won a medal in Women's Olympic Track Cycling in two decades until the team captured silver at the 2012 Olympics. The team was not as well funded as others, such as the British team, which was also better staffed by a ratio of 10 to 1. When the U.S. team entered Olympics training three months before the games, it needed to close a 5-second gap to have a chance at a medal. Many team members and patrons thought this was almost impossible.

Actions: The team was guided by Sky Christopherson, who was an athlete on the U.S. Cycling Team in the 1996 and 2000 Olympic games and cofounder of the biometrics and genomics health company, Optimized Athlete. For 24 hours of every day, the team collected and correlated quantified-self data from sensors and cameras, including genetics tests, environmental information, sleep patterns, blood glucose levels, blood pressure levels, and heart rate. Apart from reporting the key metrics visually, the team also profiled other drivers with metrics, such as daily activity and nutrition patterns, and early morning sun exposure training routines and their performance in each. The team did a trend analysis on the impact of changes on their performance over time.

Based on the analytics, the team formulated its race strategies, health and recovery routines, and made changes to day-to-day activity patterns and habits. In short, team members adopted all new analytics-driven recommendations to improve the health and performance of the cyclists.

Impact: The U.S. team had initially entered the games with a 5-second handicap. But it went on to beat the overwhelmingly favorite Australia by 0.08 seconds in the semifinal round and brought home the silver medal.

References

http://datameer.com/learn/videos/us-womens-olympic-cycling-team-big
   -data-story.html

fora.tv/2013/06/27/The_US_Womens_Cycling_Teams_Big_Data_Story

//enhancedkinetics.com/interviews/sky-christopherson-biometric-hacking/

www.wired.com/2012/06/insidetracker/

www.dailymail.co.uk/news/article-2177666/London-2012-Olympic-athletes
   -swap-personal-fitness-data-latest-gadgets-bid-2012-edge.html

Case Study 3: Fighting Crime in Memphis

Situation: Memphis was considered one of the most crime-ridden cities in the United States in 2005. As a result, University of Memphis professor Richard Janikowski began to work with the Memphis Police Department to developed and implement a predictive analytics tool that would create a model to fight crime. The initiative was called Operation Blue Crush.

Actions: The core strategy was to use crime statistics to identify places and times with a high probability of crime. The Memphis Police Department had already been gathering and mapping data on every reported crime. Operation Blue Crush used that data to model and create maps of "focus areas" and to create drivers, such as time of day and day of week. When the model shows a pattern of possible activity, police reinforcements were then sent to proactively prevent or mitigate the incidence of a crime on a real-time basis. The police department could also deploy resources from different crime fighting units, such as organized crime, special operations, traffic, and DUI enforcement.

The department's data collection was enhanced when officers were given hand-held devices that enabled them to file reports on the spot, creating a readily accessible database for officers on the move.

Impact: In the first 7 years of the program, from 2005 to 2012, violent crime decreased by 23 percent and burglaries in Memphis dropped five times more than the national average. An IBM case study estimated that Memphis achieved an 863 percent return on its investment, calculated as the cost of additional forces that would have been required to bring about this decline in crime without the help of analytics.

References

http://www.commercialappeal.com/news/2010/sep/19/blue-crush-gives
-ibm-a-boost/

http://www.memphispolice.org/BLUE%20Crush.htm

http://www.commercialappeal.com/news/2013/jan/27/blue-crush
-controversy/

wreg.com/2013/05/01/the-brain-behind-operation-blue-crush-retires/

Case Study 4: Controlling Outbreaks of Disease

Situation: Manitoba is the largest pork-exporting province in Canada; its largest client is the United States. An unmanaged disease outbreak among pigs could be financially catastrophic to Manitoba's pork export industry. Traditionally, the Manitoba Agriculture, Food and Rural Initiatives ministry collected data about potential outbreaks by word of mouth from various sources, including farmers, laboratory personnel, and veterinarians, to develop strategies for preventing and controlling animal disease outbreaks.

Actions: In 2010, the Ministry instituted an electronic tracking system that uses premises identification to track the movement of livestock. Soon after launch of the tracking system, they detected a transmittable gastroenteritis (TGE) outbreak in pigs within a cluster of three farms.

The database collected information on the livestock. Visualization of disease trackers helped to quickly locate the outbreak, determine the size of outbreak, and view the movement of the infected livestock. Through analysis, they were able to calculate potential exposure zones outside of the infected areas. Predictive models helped assess the severity of the outbreak. What-if scenario planning helped understand potential patterns of spread of the disease, and the strategies that could be deployed to address them. Correlation analysis helped identify exposed animals that had come into and out of the affected farms.

Impact: By quickly identifying and analyzing the risks, the disease control time period was reduced by 80 percent. No additional farms were affected by the TGE outbreak, and the risk of export restrictions was drastically reduced. This prevented cull-related losses amounting to millions of dollars.

References

http://www.ibm.com/smarterplanet/us/en/leadership/mafri/assets/pdf/
    MAFRI_Paper.pdf

http://www.ibm.com/smarterplanet/us/en/leadership/mafri/

Case Study 5: Outing J. K. Rowling

Situation: A first-time author, Robert Galbraith, had written a crime novel called *The Cuckoo's Calling*. The UK *Sunday Times* received an anonymous tip on Twitter claiming that Galbraith was actually J. K. Rowling, the author of the *Harry Potter* series.

Actions: Before confirming this with the publisher, the *Sunday Times* arts editor, Richard Brooks, had his team members do some sleuthing and discovered that the two authors did indeed share the same publisher and agent. They consulted two computer scientists to confirm whether *The Cuckoo's Calling* and Rowling's books showed linguistic similarities.

Forensic linguistics leverages statistical analyses to mine texts, blogs, tweets, and Amazon reviews for clues about authors. Writers choose words to convey specific messages, but these words carry signature information they don't realize they're putting out. The computer scientists were given the text of five books to test the above hypothesis, one book each from four known authors and one by Rowling called *The Casual Vacancy*.

In the first analysis, each sequence of tens of thousands of words in a book were run through the computer program, JGAAP, which compared *Cuckoo* to the other books using four different analyses, each focused on a different aspect of writing. One compared word pairings, or sets of adjacent words. For example, it would show the types of things an author describes as "expensive": a car, clothes, food, and so on. A second test searched for "character n-grams," or sequences of adjacent characters. For example, a search for the sequence "jump" would show jump, jumps, jumped, and jumping. A third test focused on most common words—words like a, and, of, and the. Looking at the 100 most common words in each book and comparing differences in frequency showed that one word might show up 5 percent of the time for one author and 7 percent of the time for another. The fourth test just looked at word lengths to analyze what percentage of the book was made up of three-letter words, four-letter words, and so on. This fourth test showed a pattern that was very characteristically Rowling.

Another scientist performed a second analysis on eight books, getting an additional book from each of the four authors. These eight books and *Cuckoo* were analyzed using a linguistics software program called Signature. All the books were compared on six features: word length, sentence length, paragraph length, letter frequency, punctuation frequency, and word usage. *Cuckoo* turned out to be most similar to a known Rowling book on four such tests.

Impact: Once Brooks was fairly confident that the Twitter tipster was right, he reached out to Rowling and in time received confirmation that she indeed was the author.

References
phenomena.nationalgeographic.com/2013/07/19/how-forensic-linguistics
-outed-j-k-rowling-not-to-mention-james-madison-barack-obama-and
-the-rest-of-us/

Case Study 6: Behind Our Title,
Behind Every Good Decision

Situation: We are subject matter experts in analytics, yes. But, as first-time authors, we were drinking from the fire hose to learn about book writing and the publishing process. A big challenge was to decide on a title for our book, one that would attract our target audience's attention and invite readers to purchase the book.

Actions: A title that caught our attention then was Tim Grahl's *First 1000 Copies: The Step-by-Step Guide to Marketing Your Book* (Out:think Group, 2013), with a complete section on how to determine a book title. Grahl's book title was so relevant to our need that it only took us three seconds to decide to buy his book. The data-driven process he outlined resonated with us, and we adapted his process for our search for the best book title.

1. Using Facebook, Twitter, and LinkedIn, we asked our target audience for ideas for a book title based on a description of the book. These ideas were combined with a list produced from our internal team's brainstorming sessions.
2. From this main list, 45 options were shortlisted.
3. We asked our target audience to vote, and thus we narrowed it down to the top eight titles.
4. We used a service called PickFu to design a series of A/B tests. We leveraged PickFu's feature that surveyed audience members about why they made a specific choice. With this information, we tweaked the final list of main title and subtitle combinations. Pickfu got us down to the top four titles, but no further. When we sliced the poll results for the top four titles using our target demographic, the numbers were small and thus the results were insignificantly different between options A and B. We needed the capabilities of another tool to finalize the winner.
5. We moved the testing and polls to Google Adwords, where we showed the top four main title and subtitle combinations to any user who typed our target search keywords (analytics, business analytics, etc.) and decided on the one that got us the highest click-through rate.

Impact: *Behind Every Good Decision* won by a big margin over several other titles, including *Adding Precision to Your Decision, Minimizing Analytics, Maximizing Results,* and others. It resulted in four times the click-through rate than the second choice, *The Guide to Business Analytics.* We also created buzz with our target audience by involving them in this decision making. So, thank you, Tim Grahl and analytics!

Case Study 7: A Google Innovation Secret

Situation: Within 10 years of its IPO, Google has become the second most valuable firm in the world. Its success can be attributed to the extraordinary people it attracts, retains, and nurtures. Google accomplishes this with unique people management practices based on "people analytics." It believes maximizing innovation is possible only with the best innovators on board.

Actions: Human Resources (HR) at Google uses data-based processes for making decisions concerning staffing. The people analytics team has a person embedded in each HR group reporting directly to the VP of HR. They conduct analyses, generate insights, and provide recommendations. Some exceptional HR policies with origins in analytics are the following.

1. **Good vs. great managers**: "Project Oxygen" analyzed a ton of data to determine that great managers were critical for retention and top performance of the workforce. The analyses also identified eight characteristics of great managers as opposed to just good managers. These included periodic one-on-one coaching and frequent personalized feedback, which were valued much more than technical knowledge. Today, managers are rated twice a year by their employees on those eight factors.

2. **Happy and healthy**: Google's PiLab conducts experiments to determine ways to maintain a productive environment. Health being a key factor in productivity, the lab found that Google could encourage employees to reduce calorie intake in the cafeteria to stay healthy simply by reducing the size of the plates in the cafeteria.

3. **The recruit**: Google has a scientific approach to hiring and has even developed an algorithm to predict which candidates have the highest probability of success. Analysis also indicated that there was very little value added after four interviews of

potential employees, thereby significantly reducing the time to hire.

4. **Good versus best:** HR analytics has proven that there is a 300-fold performance difference between an exceptional technologist and an average one. Proving this value has helped to get resources required to hire, retain, and develop exceptional technical talent.

5. **Workplace design to drive collaboration:** Google's data showed that increased innovation came from a combination of three factors: learning, collaboration, and fun, so Google's workplace is designed to maximize these. In fact, the company even tracks time spent by employees in the cafeteria lines to maximize collaboration!

6. **Increasing discovery and learning:** Google knows that the majority of people learn on the job. So, rather than focus on traditional classroom learning, the company emphasizes hands-on learning, increasing project rotations, learning from failures, and inviting people like Al Gore and Lady Gaga to speak to their employees.

Impact: Google employees have an amazing workforce productivity that few can match. On average each employee generates $1 million in revenue each year.

Reference
http://tlnt.com/2013/02/26/how-google-is-using-people-analytics-to
 -completely-reinvent-hr/

Case Study 8: Reversing the High School Dropout Rate in Hamilton County

Situation: Hamilton County in Tennessee saw that students were consistently scoring below state benchmarks and standardized tests and had very high dropout rate. Administrators realized they could act if they understood the contributing factors.

Actions: Dr. Kirk Kelly, the Director of Accountability and Testing, realized that dropout rates and lagging performance needed to be tackled at the individual student level. The challenge was to identify the at-risk students before their problems led them to drop out. But the warning signs were often so complex and cumulative in nature that it made it hard for teachers to track and observe them.

Kelly helped develop a performance modeling tool that took individual student data from the county's 78 schools and created predictive profiles that could label a student "fragile" or "off-track." The model determined which factors were strongest predictors of a student's failure and helped flag students in need of proactive intervention. The administrators used creative means to reach out to such students, even reaching out to them via Facebook.

The county has also used analytics for teacher incentive programs. Researchers looked at the historical relationship between eighth-grade test scores and high school exams to predict a baseline performance benchmark for each student. Teachers are then compensated based on their ability to beat this benchmark.

Impact: The graduation rate in the county increased eight points to 80 percent. Over the past few years, standardized testing scores have also increased by more than 10 percent in both math and reading.

Reference

www.ibm.com/smarterplanet/us/en/leadership/hamiltoncounty/assets/
    pdf/IBM_Hamilton_County.pdf

Case Study 9: Washing Out
Money Laundering

Situation: According to the BBC Monitoring Service, approximately $2.7 billion is laundered in Colombia each year. As a result, Colombia passed stricter reporting requirements for banks, which meant that Bancolombia, Colombia's largest private bank with more than 6 million customers, needed new approaches for analyzing its data. This was particularly challenging as the bank was in the process of acquiring a rival bank, Conavi. The organization already had rigid rules and procedures for flagging fraudulent transactions, but they could not easily be amended to detect evolving criminal practices. This resulted in significant manual work to review flagged transactions and accounts.

Actions: The bank built predictive models to detect suspicious transactions that could be related to money laundering or terrorism financing. The model analyzed two million transactions per day by key variables, such as seasonal variation, age, and occupation, to identify deviations from expected patterns for commercial and individual customer segments. The model was also capable of detecting subtle suspicious relationships between originators and beneficiaries of money, which were difficult to track manually.

Impact: The model improved the reporting of suspicious transaction by 40 percent. The model's efficiency was particularly stellar in lowering misclassification so that the manual review of transactions decreased from 120,000 to only 6,000 per year. The bank increased productivity by 80 percent and reallocated resources from transaction review to revenue generating activities, such as new business.

Reference
public.dhe.ibm.com/common/ssi/ecm/en/ytc03092usen/YTC03092USEN
.pdf

Case Study 10: From No-Go to No. 1

Situation: In 2004, energy drink company Red Bull bought Ford's Formula 1 team, Jaguar Racing, now called Infiniti Red Bull Racing. The team had not won a Formula 1 race in five years. The last best performance was in 2004, when the team came in seventh out of 11 teams.

Actions: As Red Bull analyzed the team's performance to create opportunities to improve, it gathered and looked at 100 gigabytes of data from every race. Most of this was telemetric data of cars on the move. Over 100 sensors in the cars gathered this information—temperature, g-forces, spin and more—that a team of engineers analyzed real-time in an off-track garage. The data was also sent to Red Bull's UK operations center simultaneously. The operations center had 24 analysts with four rows of screens analyzing the streaming data, not unlike a NASA mission control center.

During the race, experts on each aspect of the car synthesized the output. Armed with headsets, they connected with the drivers, engineers, and the pit crew to help the team dramatically increase reaction time to situations on the ground.

Impact: In 2012, Sebastian Vettel, Red Bull's star driver, won five of the 20 races, maintaining an exceptional lead throughout. In the final race of the season, a crash on the track might have cost Red Bull the championship. However, rather than bringing the driver to the pit to assess the damage, the team kept him on the track while engineers assessed the damage through data from the sensors. With this time saved, Vettel was able to complete the race and come in sixth, still keeping him in the lead and winning himself and his team the 2012 FIA Formula 1 World Championship.

The Infiniti Red Bull Racing team now dominates Formula 1 racing the way Ferrari did in the early 2000s with Michael Schumacher. It has won a double championship every year since 2010, one for individual driver and one for the team.

Reference

qz.com/131429/how-upstart-red-bull-racing-came-to-dominate-formula-1
    -with-superfast-internet-and-tons-of-data/

Appendix

BUSINESS STATS 101

This is a short primer on basic business statistics. Let's start with some definitions.

Population is a collection of people or things you are trying to study (i.e., "the data set"). It could be all employees at your company or all parts produced in the month of February or a specific segment of your customers.

In the business context, we aim to understand and describe characteristics of a population, such as the age of our customers. Two common descriptive parameters are average and variance (or standard deviation). Average is the measure of central tendency of that metric and standard deviation is the measure of breadth.

Average: There are three different measures of average.

1. Mean is the sum of a given set of numbers divided by the size of the set. It is the most popular measure of average for a normal distribution. Many things in our daily life roughly look like a bell curve in a normal distribution (see Exhibit A-1). For exam-

EXHIBIT A-1. Normal, Bell-Shaped Curve

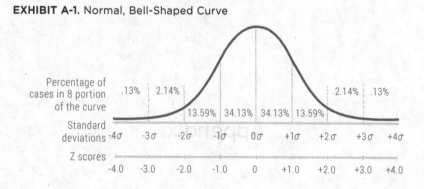

Percentage of cases in 8 portion of the curve	.13%	2.14%					2.14%	.13%
			13.59%	34.13%	34.13%	13.59%		

Standard deviations: -4σ　-3σ　-2σ　-1σ　0σ　$+1\sigma$　$+2\sigma$　$+3\sigma$　$+4\sigma$

Z scores: -4.0　-3.0　-2.0　-1.0　0　+1.0　+2.0　+3.0　+4.0

ple, for a class that starts at 8 AM, the time of arrival of students would roughly represent this curve; the mean is probably around 8 AM.

Mean is represented by µ and calculated using this formula, where n is the size of the set and X_i represents each data point.

$$\mu = \frac{\sum_{i=1}^{n} x_i}{n}$$

2. Median is the middle number (used as average when the sample has outliers).
3. Mode is the number that appears most frequently in a set of numbers. This behavior is called a modality. In a nonnormal distribution, mode is a better representation of average than mean or median. For example, if you look at the number of cars on the road, it is usually nonnormal bimodal distribution, where the numbers peak around 8 AM and 5 PM. For a city planner, knowing the mean number of cars on the street is less significant than knowing these most common frequencies of cars on the road.

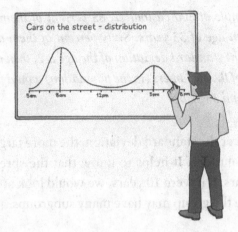

Standard Deviation

The standard deviation (σ), is the square root of variance—a measure of how far a set of numbers is spread out from the mean (μ). It is used to describe the spread of a data set and calculated using the formula:

$$\sigma = \frac{\sum\limits_{i=1}^{n}(x_i-\mu)^2}{n}$$

In a situation which can be approximated to a normal distribution, knowing the mean and standard deviation allows us to approximate that 68 percent of the values fall within one standard deviation from the mean and that 95 percent of the values fall within two standard deviations of the mean (see Exhibit A-1). This is a standard property of any normal distribution. This is useful, as when we don't have known population attributes to measure the middle 68 percent, we use a known sample's standard deviation to extrapolate the spread of the population.

In aggregate analysis, we use average and standard deviation to describe a population or compare two segments. Let's revisit Gable Wines from Chapter 3.

In a sample of 300 customers, 85 percent of them are women,
with a mean age of 33 years. Sixty percent of them are staying in
Oregon. If the standard deviation of the age is 2, then we know that
68 percent of the customers (in the population) would fall within the
ages of 31 and 35 years.

The narrower the standard deviation, the more targeted our demographic and solutions. It helps to know that the spread is two years
and not 10 years. If it were 10 years, we would look at segmenting the
group because the group may have many subgroups.

Z-score

This is the technical term for describing how many standard deviations
a data value is from the mean. It is used to evaluate whether a particular point is typical or atypical. Z-score is calculated using the formula:

$$Z = \frac{X - \mu}{\sigma}$$

where *X* is the value for which you're evaluating z-score.

Mary, who is 20 years old, wants to book her wedding at Gable
Wines. Her Z-score is therefore 6.5 ((20–33)/2 = 6.5). Since she is
more than two standard deviations away from the mean, she is not
your typical customer. Let's say Mary is willing to splurge and asks
for extra amenities that you don't currently have. Just because you
know she is not a typical customer, you may not need to start invest-
ing in those extra amenities unless many of your typical customers
start asking for it.

These are the ways in which we use business statistics to make
business decisions.

Error

At Gable Wines, you are trying to compare how many people submit wedding information requests using a new short form versus the current standard form. You tested the conversion between the two forms. Let's say the short form conversion rate is 69 percent versus 65 percent for the standard form using last week's website traffic.

Do you think if you showed the forms to next week's visitors, your numbers would be exactly the same? Likely not. This is because as you sample from a population, it comes with a variance—that is, there is statistical error. Error is a function of sample size, sample proportion or standard deviation, and Z-critical, a constant. If we want to be 95 percent confident, we use a Z-critical of 1.96 (Refer to Exhibit A-1 for a normal distribution graph).

So, in order to say that the conversion difference of 69 percent versus 65 percent from the first week of the test is truly meaningful, the percentage difference needs to be greater than the error. Let's say, for the forms, we find by formula that the error rate is 2 percent. Since the difference of 4 percent is greater than error rate, we can say with 95 percent confidence, that the short form drives higher conversion than standard form. That the difference is statistically significant. If the error were found to be 6 percent, then the 4 percent difference would be less than the error rate. Thus, there is insignificant statistical difference, meaning that the two forms convert similarly (see Exhibit A-2).

In fact, the media has played with the concept of statistical error in political reporting. According to a preelection poll reported in the U.S. presidential elections in 2012, 49 percent of likely voters said they were backing Obama, with 47 percent supporting Romney.[1] The 2 percent point margin was within the survey's sampling error, meaning the race was actually a statistical tie with no clear leader. Of course, we all know the sensationalism with which a clear leader was reported from these polls!

EXHIBIT A-2. Statistical Difference

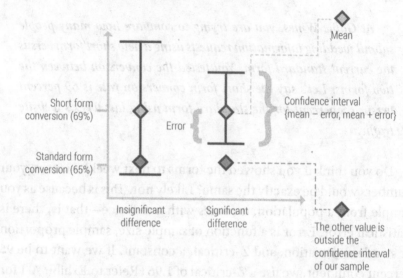

Error is calculated using the formulas given below.

Error for difference between two sample means (e.g., average age comparison between two samples) is:

$$z\sqrt{\frac{S_1^2}{n_1} + \frac{S_2^2}{n_2}}$$

In which,

n_1 and n_2 are the sample sizes, and

S_1 and S_2 are sample standard deviations.

The error rate for the difference between two sample proportions (e.g., the open rate comparison between two sample email blasts to choose the winning subject line) is determined by:

$$z\sqrt{\frac{\hat{p}_1(1 - \hat{p}_1)}{n_1} + \frac{\hat{p}_2(1 - \hat{p}_2)}{n_2}}$$

In which,

n_1 and n_2 are the sample sizes,

p_1 and p_2 are the two sample proportions (response rate), and

z is the z-critical, a multiplier dependent on confidence level (CL). (For 95 percent CL, $z = 1.96$ for large samples.)

CORRELATION

This is the statistical measure of the linear relationship between two or more random variables and is represented by **r** (the Pearson correlation coefficient) with values between +1 and −1. The closer the value is to +1 or −1, the higher is the correlation. No correlation is indicated by **r** = 0.

$$r = \frac{\sum_{i=1}^{n}(X_i - \bar{X})(Y_i - \bar{Y})}{\sqrt{\sum_{i=1}^{n}(X_i - \bar{X})^2}\sqrt{\sum_{i=1}^{n}(Y_i - \bar{Y})^2}}$$

For continuous variables, the correlation coefficient can be calculated using the above formula and can be visualized by plotting X against Y. If X increases as Y increases or X decreases as Y increases, then X is correlated to Y. The strength of correlation is indicated by **r**.

Let's explain the case for noncontinuous variables with the example table for Gable Wines below (see Exhibit A-3). For noncontinuous variables (like traffic sources) and variables in aggregate form (4 percent conversion over 7,224 visits from Google), correlation is found through cross-tabulation (conversion by traffic source). If different sources show different conversion rates (Google is 4 percent, and Bing is 1 percent) and the difference is statistically significant, then the two variables (source and conversion) are said to have some correlation. This directly indicated which sources are yielding good results—like wineryweddingguide.com and weddingwire.com. Marketing spending can be reallocated accordingly.

EXHIBIT A-3. Gable Wines: Conversion Table

SOURCE/MEDIUM	VISITS	FORM CONVERSION
google/organic	14,440	4%
google/cpc	7,224	4%
Bing/cpc	4,360	1%
(direct)/(none)	3,651	2%
myportlandwedding.com/	2,546	5%
facebook.com/referral	1,505	0%
bing/organic	962	4%
yahoo/organic	628	5%
stinnocentwine.com/referral	488	4%
wineryweddingguide.com/	437	10%
weddingwire.com/referral	381	11%
eolaamityhills.com/referral	370	0%
apps.facebook.com/referral	256	0%
vibranttable.com/referral	146	8%
google.com/referral	138	7%
Others-long tail	2,641	3%
Average	40,174	3%

Notes

CHAPTER 1

1. http://www.executiveblueprints.com/tips/090222circuitcity.htm
2. www.time.com/time/business/article/0,8599,1858079,00.html
3. brendname.blogspot.com/2012/03/procter-gamble-procter-gamble-co.html
4. http://www.informationweek.com/global-cio/interviews/pg-turns-analysis-into-action/231600959
5. practicalanalytics.wordpress.com/2012/03/05/roi-on-analytics-now-we-have-numbers/

CHAPTER 2

1. listosaur.com/history/5-valuable-shipwrecks-discovered-in-u.s.-waters.html
2. techblog.netflix.com/2012/04/netflix-recommendations-beyond-5-stars.html
3. www.forbes.com/sites/markfidelman/2013/10/15/meet-the-growth-hacking-wizard-behind-facebook-twitter-and-quoras-astonishing-success

CHAPTER 3

1. Answers: 1-correlation; 2-size; 3-trend; 4-aggregate; 5-aggregate; 6-customer life cycle; 7-correlation, predictive, or segmentation; 8-segmentation.

CHAPTER 4

1. Test of Significance is explained in Appendix under "Error."

CHAPTER 5

1. All names and incidents related to the Santa Cruz police department have been changed to protect the privacy of participants. Information is based on an interview by Aryng with Zach Friend of the SCPD.
2. However, we are not in favor of using predictive analytics all the time. Later in the chapter, we will share guidelines on when to use this technique and when not to use it.
3. www.netflixprize.com/
4. www.smartdatacollective.com/tedcuzzillo/118296/big-data-big-hype -big-danger
5. This and many such resources are available to you at www.aryng.com/ BABook

CHAPTER 7

1. The Capital One case study used throughout this chapter is based on hbr.org/search/Michael%20Rierson/0 Michael Rierson; Source: Stanford Graduate School of Business; 26 pages. Publication Date: Mar 02, 2007. Prod. #: M316-PDF-ENG; hbr.org/product/capital-one-leveraging -information-based-marketing/an/M316-PDF-ENG
2. www.mckinsey.com/insights/business_technology/big_data_the_next _frontier_for_innovation
3. *Ibid.*
4. newsroom.accenture.com/news/accenture-study-finds-us-workers -under-pressure-to-improve-skills-but-need-more-support-from -employers.htm

CHAPTER 8

1. www.balancedscorecard.org
2. BCG growth matrix.

CHAPTER 10

1. Jennifer Wadsworth, Bill Sherry Readies the New San Jose Convention Center, Metroactive, Metro, Silicon Valley, CA, Volume 29, No 23, Page 16, August 21, 2013. www.metroactive.com/features/san-jose-convention -center-bill-sherry.html

APPENDIX

1. http://politicalticker.blogs.cnn.com/2012/08/24/cnn-poll-obama-49 -romney-47-among-likely-voters/. This is a short stat 101 section; download the detailed Business Statistics 101 primer from aryng.com/BABook

Index

About the Authors

Piyanka Jain is President and CEO of Aryng, a management consulting company focused on analytics for business impact. As a highly regarded industry thought leader in analytics, she has been a keynote speaker at business and analytics conferences, including the American Marketing Association, Predictive Analytics World, GigaOm, and the Google Analytics User Conference. She speaks about data-driven decision making to gain competitive advantage. In 15 years as an analytics leader, she has had a more than $150 million demonstrated impact on business. As a gifted problem solver, she seeks out patterns and insights to drive change in her client's organizations and impact top levers of business. She considers customer satisfaction, empowerment, and positive engagement as the highest rewards, and dollar impact as a natural consequence of it.

She has two masters degrees; her theses focused on applied mathematics and statistics. A hiker, runner, and yogi, she lives in Sunnyvale, California, with her husband, Parth, and her daughter, Jia.

Connect with Piyanka Jain at:
Twitter: @AnalyticsQueen
Blog: www.aryng.com/blog/
Email: pj@aryng.com

Puneet Sharma is Vice President of Analytics, Growth Hacking and User Research at Move Inc. He is passionate about leveraging analytics and consumer insights for driving significant business impact.

He is a creative, awards-winning senior leader with a 15-year track record of spearheading highly effective marketing and product strategy initiatives in financial services and Internet companies. His expertise lies in driving strategy through consumer insights and deep analytics and by providing actionable recommendations for effective change execution.

After completing his MBA from University of Maryland, Puneet held marketing, product, and analytics leadership roles in Fortune 500 companies, such as PayPal, Capital One, and HSBC, where he has led consumer-based retail businesses to capture lucrative and previously unclaimed opportunities. He lives in Sunnyvale, California, with his wife and two sons.

Connect with Puneet Sharma at:
Email: puneet08@gmail.com

Printed in the USA
CPSIA information can be obtained
at www.ICGtesting.com
JSHW031938070124
54775JS00008BA/28